WILD ABOUT HARRY

WILD ABOUT HARRY

Everything You Have Ever Wanted to Know
about the Truman Scholarship

Edited by Suzanne McCray and Tara Yglesias
National Association of Fellowships Advisors

Foreword by Secretary Madeleine K. Albright

THE UNIVERSITY OF ARKANSAS PRESS
FAYETTEVILLE
2021

ISBN: 978-1-68226-171-2
eISBN: 978-1-61075-747-8

25 24 23 22 21   5 4 3 2 1

Manufactured in the United States of America

♾ The paper used in this publication meets the minimum requirements
of the American National Standard for Permanence of Paper for Printed
Library Materials Z39.48-1984.

Cataloging-in-Publication Data on file at the Library of Congress

In memory of Mr. Louis Blair (1939–2020),
a change agent of extraordinary measure

Contents

III. Why Does It Matter?

Acknowledgments

The Truman Foundation has joined with the National Association of Fellowships Advisors (NAFA) to create this volume in order to support students and their advisors as they negotiate the waters of the Truman application process. Informed advice is essential if advisors are to serve students effectively. This book is the first in what will hopefully be a series of introspectives focused on individual scholarships. It specifically focuses on various aspects of applying for the Truman Scholarship—its history, the nuts and bolts of the various aspects of the written application, key insights concerning the finalist interview, the selection process, and the potential value to the applicant as well as the scholar. A great deal of work goes into creating such a volume and the authors appreciate the efforts of those who helped make this happen.

Special thanks go to the officers and board of trustees of the Harry S. Truman Scholarship Foundation, including Secretary Madeleine K. Albright, who serves as the president of the Truman Foundation and who has also generously written a foreword for this volume. The executive secretaries of the Truman Foundation—Louis Blair, Andrew Rich, and Terry Babcock-Lumish—not only contributed essays to the volume but were instrumental in creating the transparent, applicant-focused environment from which this volume grew. Thanks to the members of the Truman Finalist Selection Committee, regional review panels, and Truman faculty representatives past and present for providing (sometimes unwittingly) material for these essays. This work would also not have been possible without the support of foundation staff past and present: Tonji Wade, program officer; Ellen Dunlavey, program manager; Rachael Johnson, communications and development officer; and former program managers Andrew Kirk and Kelsea Cooper. A special thanks to Mary Denyer, assistant secretary and head of scholarship administration for the Marshall

Aid Commemoration Commission for contributing feedback to many of these essays.

The support of NAFA has been critical to the publication of various proceedings on the topics connected with the work advisors do to support students through a competitive application process and now to this volume in support of those applying for the Truman Scholarship. We would like to thank the board members: Craig Filar (Florida State University), president; Cindy Schaarscmidt (University of Washington, Tacoma), vice president; Jeff Wing (Virginia Commonwealth University), treasurer; Robyn Curtis (Clemson University), secretary; Kelly Thornburg (University of Iowa); Laura Clippard (Middle Tennessee State University); Brian Davidson (Claremont McKenna College); Jacob English (Georgia State University); Megan Friddle (Emory University); Kim Germain (University of Illinois at Chicago); Anne Moore (Tufts University); Elizabeth Romig (American University); Anne Wallen (University of Kansas); Babs Wise (Duke University); and John Mateja (Barry Goldwater Scholarship and Excellence in Education Foundation).

Thanks go as well to the authors and to the staff of the University of Arkansas Office of Nationally Competitive Awards, especially Jonathan Langley and Emily Wright, who are both associate directors for that office. The support of the University of Arkansas's chancellor Joseph Steinmetz, provost Charles Robinson, and dean Brian Primack of the College of Education and Health Professions were important to the creation of this volume. Thanks also go to Michael Hevel, chair of the department of Rehabilitation, Human Resources, and Communication Disorders, who helped make this publication possible. Finally, thanks to the University of Arkansas Press team: Michael Bieker, director and publisher; David Scott Cunningham, editor-in-chief; and Liz Lester, production manager.

Foreword

In 1975, President Gerald Ford signed into law bipartisan legislation that established The Harry S. Truman Scholarship Foundation. Rather than being memorialized on our National Mall with a traditional granite or marble monument, it was President Truman's idea to have his presidential legacy take the unprecedented form of a living memorial. The Truman Foundation is the Presidential Monument to public service.

I readily accepted the invitation to serve as president of the Truman Foundation beginning in 2002 because it combined two things I love: President Truman and the opportunity to support young people committed to careers in public service. Truman was serving in the White House when my family immigrated to the United States, so my connection to him is personal. As my first American president, he holds a special place in my heart.

Today, the Truman Foundation continues to inspire public service. With each passing year, it seeks to meet the current moment, extending the legacy of President Truman in meaningful ways. Forty-five years after its creation, the foundation has selected more than 3,300 Truman Scholars, who have come from every state and United States territory. They have created a vibrant community of alumnae that continue to impact the world.

Both at home and abroad, Truman Scholars are on the front lines of public health and medicine, the continuing struggle for justice and equality, the preservation of the environment, the education of our citizenry, and the fundamental preservation of our democratic values and institutions. As President Truman envisioned, Truman Scholars serve in all levels of government, both in the military and in civilian capacities. Scholars come from a wide variety of disciplines, philosophies, and backgrounds, but they all share a core commitment to making our world a better place.

The Truman Foundation looks to the future with its work and makes an investment in the passions and talents of young leaders. I enjoy spending time with each new class of Truman Scholars when they come to Washington. They inspire me and make me optimistic about what lies ahead for our nation.

The Truman Scholarship has developed and changed over time—and will continue to do so. Year after year, the organization works to be known for transparency and equity. It is something the foundation wants to do to live up to the ideals of public service that the program was created to celebrate and support. In that spirit, the Truman Foundation was an early supporter of the National Association of Fellowships Advisors and its sustained efforts to make scholarships such as the Truman available and attainable for a more diverse array of students.

The essays in this book represent one way in which the Truman Foundation is striving to make its work more accessible and reach a wider pool of potential applicants. I hope these essays allow people to see the heart of a program that was rooted in Harry Truman's pragmatism, and that strives to better our world by investing in Americans stepping forward to answer the call of service.

Secretary Madeleine K. Albright

WILD ABOUT HARRY

Introduction

Since its inception, the Harry S. Truman Scholarship Foundation, through the scholarship it annually awards, has been a leader in supporting a culture of public service among undergraduate students as they launch into graduate training and their professional careers. The first class of Truman Scholars included a future governor and a future executive secretary of the Truman Foundation, as well as other distinguished and dedicated public servants. And that was only the beginning. Other notable Truman Scholars include names we know (Neil Gorsuch, Stacy Abrams, Chris Coons, Susan Rice, Janet Napolitano, Michelle Alexander, John King) and many more we do not, serving in political office or the military, making a difference in government agencies, creating or advancing nonprofits, conducting needed research, shaping the future through public and higher education, informing public opinion through various media, and addressing healthcare issues. Truman Scholars are widely known as "change agents," energetic leaders who work across political, educational, social, and generational divides. The Truman Foundation, through the Truman Scholars Leadership Week (TSLW), its internship programs, and academic and career advising, helps young scholars understand the power and institutional structures that both generate and limit change.

This scholarship, attracting vibrant, passionate, and already accomplished leaders early on, has become an eagerly sought opportunity by students who hope to join a community of like-minded future public servants. Students and universities have been "wild about Harry" since that first class of scholars. And so we come to the purpose of this book—the first in a series about individual scholarships—how do universities best help prepare their students to apply for the Truman Scholarship? Universities are themselves (for the most part) nonprofit institutions, that have as part of their responsibilities the shaping of an educated citizenry who will understand and address the common good. They provide

3

students with a variety of opportunities that encourage intellectual, social, and leadership development no matter what the student's career path may be. Such development occurs prior to (during and after) the submission of an application. This book assumes a high level of student engagement as a basic foundation on which the guidance through the Truman application process must necessarily sit. In short, the student must have demonstrated potential prior to applying. The application process can help provide a student with time for important reflection, and it can even give a student a new sense of direction or vision of possible service, but it cannot create out of whole cloth a student who will become the exceptional agent for positive change that is so central to the Truman Scholarship vision. *Wild about Harry* does not offer in any chapter (including Louis Blair's "The Truman Scholarship: Having A Winner Every Time") a formula for helping students win a scholarship. What it does is provide students and those who advise them with an understanding of what the Truman Scholarship Foundation has to offer engaged student leaders planning a career in public service, as well as how applicants might best think about their own experiences, putting them in a context that is readily comprehensible for a reader meeting them for the first time on paper.

The Truman Foundation has been eager to give students the tools they need to present themselves and their work effectively. Their efforts to make the application process transparent have a long history, which includes their interactions with Truman faculty representatives, information available on their webpage, an active Twitter account, and a policy of answering questions throughout the application process. The Truman Foundation has not waited for others to seek information out. Executive secretaries have made it a point to visit campuses across the country. In 1996, the foundation gathered a small group of Truman faculty representatives in Roanoke, Virginia, to discuss how best to support students in the process. As the benefits to such a meeting spread, a larger group met in 1997 in Philadelphia, Pennsylvania, followed by an expanded Truman and Marshall meeting for advisors in 1999 in Fayetteville, Arkansas. That meeting led to the formation (with the Truman Foundation a strong voice in the development committee) of the National Association of Fellowships Advisors (NAFA), which includes over a thousand members today. The Truman Foundation, with an eye to a larger good, wanted the group to support students in a range of disciplines applying for a variety of awards to support their goals. NAFA conducts national conferences biennially and regional ones on the off years. The Truman Foundation is always active at these events, presenting workshops and papers. There has been a publication or two from members of the foundation in all seven of the previous NAFA proceedings. These varied efforts have broadened access to the Truman scholarship process, increased the number of universities to have scholars for the first time, and allowed a level of understanding about the process that has led to a greater diversity in the scholarship pool and in those who have benefited from the process, including those selected as finalists and scholars.

Truman is not alone, of course, in its efforts to increase access. In 2002, leaders of a long list of scholarship foundations gathered in Bellagio, Italy, to discuss shared values, goals, and responsibilities. A collection of essays developed out of that meeting, *The Lucky Few and the Worthy Many: Scholarship Competitions and the World's Future Leaders* (Indiana University Press, 2004). The editors Alice Stone Ilchman (Watson Fellowship Foundation), Warren Ilchman (Soros Fellowship Foundation), and Mary Tolar (Truman Scholarship Foundation) included an essay (later reprinted in *Beyond Winning: National Scholarships Competitions and the Student Experience,* University of Arkansas, 2005) that explained persuasively why access is so critical:

> As citizens in societies concerned with merit, we believe that talent is broadly, even randomly, distributed, but only selectively developed. Because many able, talented people have not had the privilege of selective development—experiences that make candidates more attractive and available to those who select them—we are concerned that we may be missing many qualified individuals, often from groups underrepresented in many ways in our societies. Missing their potential contributions deprives not only them but all of us. It seems worthwhile to enlarge the pool even at the expense of having more disappointed people—those worthy but unchosen.

This powerful sentiment has often been quoted or alluded to in articles in NAFA volumes. Advisors want their work not only to reward and launch exceptional students, but also to lift those who have not benefited as much from that selective development. Given that scholarships reward those who have actively engaged in the classroom, on the campus, and in the community, there is a privilege and an accumulation of at least relative advantage that has accrued to all competitive applicants. They simply could not be competitive otherwise. The Truman Foundation, with an eye to lift as much as this framework allows, has broadened its pool of worthy applicants by allowing an additional number of nominees (up to three more as of the 2021 competition, to the traditional four normally allotted to four-year institutions) if the additional nominees are transfer students, opening a wider door for students who first attend community colleges.

Another way to grant access is to make application expectations clearer to all. Insider information contributes to an overwhelming advantage for a lucky few. The goal of this book is to provide advisors and students (including those who may not have access to an advisor) one more avenue of access to this "insider" information.

Wild about Harry: Everything You Have Ever Wanted to Know about the Truman Scholarship is a collection of essays by Truman Foundation members and advisors, including new essays alongside updated versions of those previously published in NAFA proceedings. The book is divided into three sections: "The Truman Scholar Community," "Applying for the Truman Scholarship," and "Why Does It Matter?" The first of these, "The Truman Scholar Community," presents the overall vision of the Truman Foundation—the scope of the legislation that created the Truman Foundation as a living memorial, opportunities it provides for scholar engagement in addition to funding, the community it encourages, and the guidance it offers to new scholars as they prepare for a future as public leaders. "Applying for the Truman Scholarship" focuses on the application process itself. Essays align with the chronology of the process, following the order of key questions in the application, then moving to the interview, and then to the moment when it is all over but the shouting. This section will be read and reread by advisors and students alike both for the jauntily written prose and for the pragmatic and spot-on advice it provides. "Why Does It Matter?" explains how the time spent in reflection as the application demands contributes to a student's development and to a clearer sense of direction.

Terry Babcock-Lumish sets the stage, in Chapter 1, "Truman Scholars: A Living Memorial," for the essays that follow. Babcock-Lumish is new to the Truman Scholarship Foundation as its most recent (and first female) executive secretary, but she is not new to the program. Selected as a Truman Scholar in 1996, she has been actively involved in the selection of scholars since 2003. She provides an interesting précis of the program's history, and even more importantly provides observations as a scholar and as a selector of scholars into what it means to apply for, receive, then fill the big shoes of the award. Finally, speaking as the foundation's head, she situates the importance of the scholarship in the context of current national and global issues.

Andrew Rich, fifth executive secretary of the Truman Foundation from 2011 to 2019, follows this detailed backdrop with an analysis of a specific opportunity the program provides. In Chapter 2 "Broadening Horizons and Building Community: The Truman Foundation's Summer Institute," Rich explains how the program moved from a focus on the scholarship itself to one on the community of scholars. Summer Institute, as most advisors know, brings Truman Scholars to DC to participate in an eight-week internship program. For many scholars, Rich tells us, SI is the highlight of their Truman experience. Rich persuasively outlines its goals. Not only do scholars earn valuable work experience in key offices in DC, meeting distinguished players in their fields, but they also reflect (an important word in the Truman lexicon) on their long-term place in public service and the right graduate program (not necessarily the most famous one) that will help them obtain it. With horizons broadened and a community of like-minded friends embraced, these more experienced and better-informed scholars are ready to make choices "with an entirely new perspective on public practice and policy."

Tara Yglesias, a long-serving and ever quick-witted deputy executive secretary of the Truman Foundation, builds on the theme of scholar community development in Chapter 3, "The Truman Scholarship Community: Unconventional Scholarship Serving the Public Good." Yglesias's discussion about the community offers overt advice on how to understand the Truman Scholarship selection process, stressing how the potential to be a good fit for the Truman Scholar community makes a finalist a more attractive candidate. There are many, many ways to be a good fit and if chosen, many, many opportunities to contribute to the Truman community. Yglesias makes clear that there is no favorite career path or personality type that wins the day; but there is always an eye to what a candidate might add to the whole. The foundation does not seek out (though would likely welcome) future famous politicians or thought influencers but rather those who are truly going to make a difference to others—those who are intent on serving the public good. Whether that is from the limelight or behind the scenes does not seem to matter, but big ambition (regardless of area) and energy do.

Andy Rich is back in Chapter 4, "Public Service, Power, and the Challenges Facing Future Public Servants," to issue a charge to advisors to engage students "around questions of power, politics, service, and democracy." Students have become disenchanted with political polarization and governmental lethargy. They want to make a difference sooner rather than later, and the glacial pace of the institutional world seems less and less attractive. Rich points out that millennials (and now Gen Z), though service-minded, distrust the traditional avenues for service. They seem more interested in challenging power than wielding it. But their hearts are in it and that gives Rich (and us) hope that if they can be persuaded back to government service, they will shake things up for the better.

Now to Part II, "Applying for the Truman Scholarship," where six of the seven essays are written by Tara Yglesias. The essays are funny and incredibly helpful for those advising students through the process. Chapter 5, "Suspenders and a Belt: Overpreparation and the Overachiever," sets the tone for the section both with its humor—Yglesias invariably has the reader laughing and taking notes at the same time—and with its message: "Let students be themselves." Assist, inform, and advise, but do not overwhelm the spark that is the student's own. Yglesias expresses comic, but real dismay at the "overscripted," "overwrought," and "overwhelmed" finalists who too often appear at interviews. These finalists seem to be rehearsing a script rather than engaging in a conversation. This chapter reminds advisors and students that being authentic is a welcomed trait. There are times when less is more.

In Chapter 6, "Non Ducor, Duco: Leadership and the Truman Application," Tara Yglesias waggishly outlines what leadership does not mean to reviewers (as she trains these reviewers, she has great credibility in this). Though not the end-all of the application, leadership is clearly an important aspect of an applicant's record. What then are the key elements for Truman? Leadership by example? No. Leadership as mentoring? No. Leadership by committee? No. Leadership by doing a really great job? Again, no. Knowing what leadership is not for Truman is certainly helpful, but knowing what Truman considers it to be is even more so, and Yglesias provides the essential elements of what leadership is and explains how to frame experiences in that context for applicants wishing to declare *non ducor, duco.*

The Truman Scholarship funds graduate school for these future leaders—that is, of course, the scholarship part of the award. Scholars can defer using the scholarship for four years (or more with permission). They can change their minds about what degree and what school they choose (the Truman Foundation often weighs in on this with those selected). Some actually never find time to use it, but all must detail a plan (for now) in the application. In Chapter 7, "I Love It When a Grad Plan Comes Together: Graduate School Advising and the Truman Application," Yglesias advises candidates to think carefully (not grandly, narrowly, indiscriminately, or rigidly) about the programs they choose. Much of the essay is spent sharing what can go wrong in this section of the application (it turns out, there is a lot that can), but it also provides helpful suggestions about how students can consider a plan that is appropriate to their preparation and their planned career path. Students who want to be on the graduate school A-Team will want to read this essay with care.

Chapter 8, "When the Abyss Stares Back: The Eldritch Horror of the 'Additional Information' Prompt," is a more than six-thousand-word essay about a four-hundred-word response to what was at one time an optional question. This would seem to promise an essay that will overexplain a straightforward and perhaps even inessential aspect of the application—in short, be tedious to read. But the title (like all of Yglesias's titles, including the one for this book) promises something far more adventurous. Horror movies serve as the frame as Yglesias discusses the importance of Question 14 to the application, capturing the terror students often feel when trying to answer a question that has no limits on what they might do. Advisors are also flummoxed by this question, leaving them to ask many of their own. What do "they" want? How do I advise the student? Is there a right answer, or even a better answer? Will a bit of trauma help or a dash of disaster? Should the student explain that C in Econ? No to all those questions, says Yglesias. In this essay, as in others, her approach is to share what can go wrong (a truly frightening section) and to finally press again for genuine responses that further introduce students, giving some insight into what makes them tick.

The student completes the applications persuasively with powerful examples of leadership, extensive examples of engagement on the campus and in the community, and a drive that jumps off the page. In some (but unfortunately not all) cases, the student is invited to interview. Chapter 9, "Enough about Me, What Do You Think about Me? Surviving the Truman Interview," provides a crash course in what and what not to do leading up to and during a Truman interview. And while the warnings and suggestions are applicable specifically to Truman, they make good sense for other interview situations as well.

Yglesias reminds panelists that they are an investment committee, looking for special change agents, who have a deep commitment to service and the intellectual wherewithal to thrive in graduate school. Interviews may be rigorous, but there is never a deliberate attempt to embarrass or trick a student. Interviewers want students to understand how to stand their ground, but they also genuinely want students to be themselves and to shine. Once again as with other elements of the process, Yglesias points to authenticity as key. Practice can help a student relax and learn to enjoy the conversation that characterizes a Truman interview but overprepara-tion can turn warm and interesting finalists distant and robotic, spouting memorized phrases, citing accumulated but sometimes barely relevant data, and expressing little of their own deeply held passion for service.

Paula Warrick, a former NAFA president, moves the focus from the foundation to the advisor in Chapter 10, "An Advisor's Perspective on Reading Applications for Truman." She outlines the thorough reviewer training as well as the actual reading itself. Her essay reinforces the idea that readers want to understand the applicant as fully as possible even if at times this means reading between the lines. Because of volume, readers review applications quickly, but there is a method of review that is help-ful for advisors and students to understand. Warrick's take-aways from her experiences as a reviewer should serve as a checklist for any Truman faculty representative. Her advice to encourage students to scaffold the application is excellent and will likely change the way Truman faculty representatives across the country advise.

Aptly, the final chapter on applications brings Tara Yglesias back for a curtain call. In "You Sank My Fellowship: The 'Near-Miss' Truman Application," Yglesias skillfully employs game metaphors (*Jeopardy, Wheel of Fortune, Scattergories*, etc.) throughout to reflect the sometime attitude of "tell me the rules and we will win this thing." Yglesias points out at the beginning that an application that does not advance can be derailed in one of three ways: the pool, reader malfunction, and application malfunction. She goes on to provide examples of each. Experienced advisors will likely recognize some of their own students in the application malfunction paragraphs. According to Yglesias, most advisors know even before asking for feedback where a given application is lacking. But students rarely have a sense of this, and sharing this essay while the student is working through the application might help that light come on. Students will enjoy the humor and may also take away the lessons. The essay and the section on applications end with The Game of Life, where a lot is left to chance. Advisors cannot control the odds, the reviewers, or the holes in a student's application. But they can encourage students to take time in putting together the application, to provide context about their experiences, to be thoughtful about their future, and most importantly to be themselves— win or lose.

Part III, "Why Does It Matter," puts the process in perspective. For Louis Blair, third executive secretary of the Truman Foundation, it matters very much. Blair, whose indefatigable work helped develop many of the Truman programs that support scholars (including TSLW), references an early interview survey of unsuccessful applicants as well as an ongoing survey of finalists. The results were encouraging—the process matters to students, helping them assess and reassess their future academic and career paths, hone writing and interview skills, and network with equally ambitious peers. In Chapter 12, "The Truman Scholarship: Having a Winner Every Time," Blair directly addresses advisors, providing instruction about how to make the process valuable, "a winning experience," for all who apply and for those who guide them.

Seasoned advisors Jane Morris (former NAFA president) and Betsy Vardaman (NAFA founding board) team up for the book's final essay, Chapter 13, "Giving Shape to a Future Career Path through the Truman Process." Both have written for NAFA publications before, and together they make a persuasive case that the reflective learning that is so deeply embedded in the Truman process is what makes the application a worthwhile effort for all who apply, leading to a clearer sense of purpose and career trajectory. This article serves perfectly as a summary piece for earlier essays. It touches on the book's major themes: the Truman Foundation has been mindful of encouraging public service from its beginning and continually evolves with this goal in mind; the questions in the application are designed to create a clear picture of students and their goals and to encourage reflection on service and leadership; a thoughtful approach to the application benefits both student and application; there is much more to value in the process than just the chance of winning. The worthy many apply with only a lucky few who win, so the process has to matter deeply.

There has never been a more important time since the creation of the Truman Scholarship program to encourage students to consider careers in public service. Every aspect of our lives now cries out for service-minded students to engage energetically and thoughtfully, with a global perspective, at community, state, and national levels. Perhaps they can reach their hands across the various aisles that disrupt and divide us. Perhaps when they do they will bring meaningful, sustainable change to our healthcare systems, to our environmental policies, to the social and economic benefit of all citizens. The Truman Foundation is certainly betting on it, investing each year in our future through the living memorial that is the Truman Scholarship.

Suzanne McCray
University of Arkansas

Part I

The Truman Scholar Community

1

Truman Scholars
A Living Memorial

TERRY BABCOCK-LUMISH

President Truman: A Leader for His Time

President Harry S. Truman was, to many, an improbable—even an accidental—American president. President Truman came from unpretentious stock in Missouri, finding his way into our history books not by paving his way through America's top educational institutions—he did not attend college—but via hard work and an improbable path. From farming to field artillery and haberdashery, a young Truman's path to public service was hardly preordained. In the trenches of World War I, Captain Truman never could have imagined he would find himself in the Oval Office someday.

A plainspoken midwesterner who did not run in "fancy" circles, President Truman offers lessons learned for students of American history, but perhaps more importantly, for American leadership and service. Recognizing the need for bipartisanship and taking responsibility for difficult decisions and actions, President Truman was a keen study of human behavior, be it over card games with colleagues on Capitol Hill or, far more consequentially, on the world stage. And yet, despite his becoming the most powerful person in the world, he maintained a refreshing humility and accessibility.

15

When approached by bipartisan admirers to consider his legacy, President Truman resisted a traditional brick-and-mortar monument. Instead, he encouraged a living memorial that would give life to the values of service that had animated his career. In that spirit, the Truman Foundation is a place that nurtures and supports future generations who answer the call to public service leadership as mandated by the 1975 Harry S Truman Memorial Scholarship Act:

> The Congress finds that—
> because a high regard for the public trust and a lively exercise of political talents were outstanding characteristics of the thirty-third President of the United States;
> because a special interest of the man from Independence in American history and a broad knowledge and understanding of the American political and economic system gained by study and experience in county and National government culminated in the leadership of America remembered for the quality of his character, courage, and common sense;
> because of the desirability of encouraging young people to recognize and provide service in the highest and best traditions of the American political system at all levels of government, it is especially appropriate to honor former President Harry S. Truman through the creation of a perpetual education scholarship program to develop increased opportunities for young Americans to prepare and pursue careers in public service.[1]

Accordingly, the hallmark of the Truman Foundation's work is the premier graduate fellowship in the United States for those pursuing careers as public service leaders.

The Truman Foundation's mission is to serve as a beacon for public service for young people across the United States. Our vision is of a country that deeply values public servants. As a living memorial, there is no such thing as a past-tense Truman Scholar; rather, once a Truman, always a Truman. Accordingly, the Truman Foundation has named 3,260 scholars since its inaugural class in 1977.

Applying as Individuals, Solving Problems as a Community

Upon applying during their junior year of college, aspiring Truman Scholars detail their leadership experiences and accomplishments to date.

They articulate the greatest concerns they see facing society and what role they will play to address them. They propose their ideal graduate programs and discuss how those programs will inform their trajectories five to seven years later and perhaps far beyond. While Truman applicants are often supported by caring mentors, this is an inherently independent process of reflection and recitation. It is then essential for us, as the investment committee for the Truman Foundation to understand applicants as individuals, each with their own ideas, concerns, and theories of change.

It is then understandable that applicants are highly focused on their graduate programs and plans—as they should be—and yet, those degrees are merely the beginning of a lifelong Truman Scholar experience. The scholarship award today is thirty thousand dollars, but its true value is far greater. Newly-named Truman Scholars may need to operate as if graduate school is the focus, but it is mission-critical to broaden the aperture if we are, together as a community, to live up to the expectations outlined in the original 1975 statute—and ultimately, up to President Truman's and our bipartisan founders' shared vision.

Upon being awarded a Truman Scholarship, Truman Scholars, as well as their families, faculty representatives, mentors, and university leadership, should take pride in this accomplishment. The exciting news should serve as validation of the student's accomplishments to date and potential for future leadership in service to the nation and world. The award's impact will go far beyond a few years of funding, offering a lifetime of opportunities to participate in the Truman community for shared support and problem solving.

The Truman Foundation endeavors to provide meaningful touchpoints for Truman Scholars across the course of their lives and careers. Early in a scholar's Truman experience, opportunities for engagement include the Truman Scholars Leadership Week, Summer Institute, and Truman-Albright Fellowship Program. Later examples include our Democracy and Governance Fellowship opportunities for Truman Scholars pursuing paths in electoral politics or as senior leaders in the executive branch, respectively.

These are merely the formal programs, however. Perhaps more consequential are the relationships and shared efforts that result from these catalytic convenings. When it comes to the thorniest challenges facing society—pandemics, racism, climate change, etc.—no one can solve them alone. Rather, we will require the diverse talents, ideas, and efforts of bright, dedicated leaders coming together from across experiences, backgrounds, disciplinary training, and party lines.

For this very reason, the Truman Foundation does not expect Truman Scholars to follow precisely in President Truman's footsteps. After all, he was a leader for a different time, and we need not all pursue elected office, although it is an honorable path. All Truman Scholars, however, should understand the Truman experience, history, and legacy in application to twenty-first-century challenges.

There is no one-size-fits-all for a Truman Scholar. At spring interviews, we want to see organizers engaged in #BlackLivesMatter, #NeverAgain, #MeToo, and other hashtagged movements whose names have yet to emerge. We want to meet the leaders of both College Republicans and College Democrats. We are excited to see aspiring Truman Scholars serving in uniform, as well as those aspiring to wear the robes of a federal judge or the dirt-stained or paint-splattered jeans of local leaders pursuing their path in public service through systems change in sustainable agriculture or raising awareness through public art.

Truman Scholars come from a rich diversity of nominating institutions and bring to bear experiences that are matchless. Consider what this looks like in our world, from application to many years on:

- An individual whose education-oriented application offers a veritable blueprint for his eventual path, from efforts within the classroom to leading schools, and ultimately serving at the highest levels in both state and federal education policy making
- A leader on Capitol Hill today, who has not even attended graduate school, yet is just as much a Truman Scholar, regularly mentoring and supporting a host of younger Truman Scholars as they make their way in legislative service
- A scholar who began as premed, only to course-correct to use her law degree and experience with Teach for America to become the lead teacher's union organizer for a large midwestern state
- A Republican elected official, widely known for her leadership in alternative energy and innovation policy, who collaborated successfully with a Truman Scholar then serving as a Democratic governor of a large southwestern state
- An active-duty military officer whose work as a physician-scientist

is protecting not only the American public but also society at large, as a leader in pandemic surveillance, biological threats, and global health

These individuals hail from a variety of institutions, from large state schools and service academies to community colleges and elite private schools. Truman Scholars include Native Americans and new Americans alike. They are first-generation college students and the children of lauded intellectuals. They are socioeconomically and demographically diverse, and they represent a host of lived experiences.

All campuses have students who are bundles of ambition and energy; however, to become a Truman Scholar, one must have more than a resume. Truman Scholars may or may not be first in their classes, especially if they are actively exploring new ideas and pushing their own intellectual limits or assumptions within or beyond the traditional classroom. Truman Scholars are the very people in communities who do not simply spot problems, but jump into action to solve challenges in sustainable ways. Truman Scholars have theories of change. They have ideas and move beyond dialogue to action.

Today's Challenges

As a country and as a people, the United States has weathered tumultuous times: the Civil War, the Great Depression, assassinations of political and civic leaders, and the divisiveness of Vietnam, to name just a few. Today we find ourselves at a critical inflection point in our nation's history, with our very democratic processes and institutions called into question, and tectonic technological and economic changes afoot for our workforce. We are confronting a long-overdue reckoning with systemic racism and injustice. In the midst of global demographic and political shifts, combined with unconventional weaponry and non-state actors, many are reconsidering America's role in the world. We also face ecological and epidemiological threats, which scarcely respect established political boundaries.

Accounts of American communities' polarization have been pervasive since the 2016 presidential election, but Republicans and Democrats across the nation have been moving further apart ideologically since the 1990s. Where there used to be overlap between the views of Democrats and Republicans, now there is almost none. Ninety-two percent of Republicans now sit to the right of the median Democrat, while 94 percent of Democrats sit to the left of the median Republican.[2] In Congress, the two parties thwart each other's legislation and demonize their political opponents as unpatriotic or untruthful. And Americans now see the conflicts between Democrats and Republicans as more extreme than those dividing urban and rural residents, the rich and poor, or Black and white Americans.[3]

During trying times, one naturally seeks signs of reassurance or stability. Rather than finding solace in knowing that steady hands are at the wheel, the reality is that subject matter experts across the country are readying for retirement. Over a decade ago, Pew projected a "silver tsunami" as baby boomers prepare to retire.[4] While many consider this a prime opportunity for fresh ideas and voices, concerns abound that we sit underprepared for this transition. This shift will be particularly acute within the federal workforce. In the U.S. Department of Housing and Urban Development alone, almost a quarter of all workers are currently eligible for retirement—a percentage spiking to almost half by 2023.[5]

Truman Scholars: Leaders for Our Time

The Truman change agent can step up to the challenges we face and move beyond partisan rancor and rhetoric toward constructive problem solving and healing. At this time, they are precisely the leaders we need, and our diversity is our strength. Public service is a big tent, and we need the very brightest leaders joining forces, not to address low-hanging fruit, but to dig into the toughest of the tough: nuclear threats, pandemics, climate change, inequality.

We no longer live in the William Whyte "Organization-Man" era, working a full career in a single organization and then predictably retiring.[6] To the contrary, regardless of the area of expertise, it seems most come at issues of education, health, or justice across the course of local, state, and federal government—or across the public, private, and civic sectors—at various points in their careers. It would be folly not to anticipate dynamism and change across careers, so the ability to anticipate and adapt becomes essential. Truman Scholars are the very community to help peers navigate increasingly nonlinear careers.

When it comes to problem solving in an increasingly fast-paced, global, mobile world, there is tremendous value to being well prepared as an individual, but it is essential to look beyond oneself, to anticipate challenges, and to empathize with individuals whose lived experiences are different from one's own. Current and future Truman Scholars have wildly varying dreams and plans for how they will better our world. Doing so will require both know-how and know-who.

Our job today is to build capacity to face the challenges of the day and the future. If we, as a foundation and a broader community across colleges and universities, do our job right, we will all be better off for this. President Truman and his colleagues in the 1970s could not have anticipated today's Washington—or London, Berlin, or Beijing—but their vision paved the way for a prepared community of leaders to tackle the issues of the day—today and tomorrow.

2

Broadening Horizons and Building Community
The Truman Foundation's Summer Institute

ANDREW RICH

When the first class of Truman Scholars was selected in 1977, the freshly minted scholars—all college sophomores—were flown to Independence, Missouri, for a weekend ceremony to be recognized among their peers and sent off with $20,000 in scholarship support. The money *was* the award. Back then, scholars received support for their last two years of college and the first portion of a graduate program, and they met each other only that one time. From there, they were sent off to finish their educations with independence from one another and from the Truman Scholarship Foundation.

Times have changed, and so has the Truman Scholar experience. During the past forty-plus years, the number and types of graduate programs relevant to public service have multiplied, as have the challenges facing leaders in public service. In response, the mandate of the Truman Foundation has evolved such that it not only provides financial support to an outstanding collection of individual change agents but also seeks to build community among them through programming. Community building among Truman Scholars strengthens their knowledge of the diverse paths to public service leadership; it deepens their commitment to lead and work in collaboration with others; and it forms bonds of lasting

23

friendship that inevitably provide support during challenging times, both personal and professional.

Summer Institute

The Truman Foundation's Summer Institute is central to these efforts. In the summer that occurs a year following their selection (and, therefore, typically just after they finish college), the scholars spend eight weeks in Washington, DC, participating in paid internships in the public or non-profit sectors and in a wide variety of seminars and workshops focused on professional and personal development. Scholars spend the summer living together in residence halls centrally located in downtown Washington, and foundation staff members focus on providing the group with mentoring and fellowship opportunities.

Truman Scholars arrive in Washington, DC, for Summer Institute around Memorial Day, and they spend their first week participating in workshops that acquaint them with the city, with leaders from all corners of public service, and with some of the challenges they can expect to face during the course of the summer. For example, in 2011, the first week included Q&A sessions with a Supreme Court justice, senior members of the executive branch, and Senator Chris Coons (D-DE), the first Truman Scholar elected to the U.S. Senate. Scholars participated in a simulation of congressional decision making, a workshop about arts, culture, and public policy, and—always a highlight of the week—a meal at Ben's Chili Bowl, a much-loved DC institution.

After the orientation week, scholars begin their eight-week full-time internship placements. The foundation does its best to match internship placements to scholars' interests. And thanks to the goodwill formed by the foundation's track record of providing agencies and organizations with first-rate people over the years, its scholars tend to obtain more substantive opportunities—and have more positive experiences—than many others who intern in DC.

During the period of their internships, the scholars come together every Tuesday evening for workshops planned by the scholars on a rotating basis on topics related to their professional development. The foundation also holds occasional social gatherings throughout the summer, and the scholars tend to plan many more on their own—potlucks, happy hours around the city, and road trips on the weekends. The summer ends with a half-day symposium where scholars present to one another about their summer experiences.

Truman Scholars consistently say that their participation in Summer Institute is the highlight of their Truman experience. Many come into Summer Institute with no interest in living or working in Washington, DC, over the long term; others see their arrival in Washington as the beginning of something permanent. By the end of the summer, at least as many from the former group have joined the latter as the other way around. Summer Institute is a structured opportunity for Truman Scholars to experiment professionally and grow personally.

One Truman Scholar who participated observed:

> My summer in DC proved to be a tremendous growth and network-ing opportunity. As a scholar placed at the Department of Health and Human Services' Office of Health Affairs, I was involved in a study of state animal disease response plans. My supervisors were a fantastic set of veterinarians with unique professional experiences who encouraged me to engage in other DHS and federal operations, opening my eyes to an entirely new sector of endless career potential. Summer Institute supplemented this phenomenal internship by providing interactions with outstanding leaders in other fields. I also grew closer to my fellow scholars and was humbled by their extraordinary successes. Because of Summer Institute, I entered veterinary school with an entirely new per-spective on public practice and policy.

This scholar was one of the first in the foundation's history to pur-sue a degree in veterinary science. Her choice of that graduate program and her understanding of how it connected to public service were influ-enced by her participation in Summer Institute. That is a home run in the Truman Scholarship book.

Even for those who either do not end up liking their internship place-ment or find that Washington, DC, is not the place for them, the expe-rience of being with other Truman Scholars is memorable, leaving them with lasting friendships. From the foundation's perspective and from a professional perspective, it can be as worthwhile for scholars to figure out what is not for them as it is for them to determine the paths to pursue.

Building Community for Public Service Leadership

By design the Truman Scholarship provides money for graduate education. But Truman Scholars should not go to graduate school until they have confidence about how a specific program and degree will help them in their careers. The Summer Institute is designed to help move Truman Scholars down the road to where they have clarity about the type of graduate program that is right for them. Sure, the application for the Truman Scholarship has a few questions about what graduate program applicants will attend and what jobs they will seek in public service. But most Truman Scholars who look back five years later have not followed the path outlined in their applications, and that is just fine with the foundation. The program uses the answers to those questions to assess how candidates think about their future, not to nail them down to an unalterable professional track.

Truman scholars often select more appropriate graduate programs, do better in graduate school, and remain in public service longer if they have taken time off to work and/or intern after completing their undergraduate degrees. Summer Institute encourages that break between college and graduate school. About one-quarter of each class of Summer Institute scholars receives offers to stay in their placements for a full year following the summer. And the overwhelming majority of Summer Institute scholars report deeper friendships and stronger connections with their fellow Truman Scholars as a result of spending the summer together in Washington. They form bonds, both professional and personal, that remain meaningful and important throughout their careers.

Summer Institute is not for everyone, and not all Truman Scholars participate in it. Some have other plans for the summer after they graduate, and we certainly do not require the program. During the Truman Scholar selection process, candidates' interest in Summer Institute has no effect on their likelihood of being selected. From one year to the next, roughly three-quarters of each cohort participate, and those who do so enjoy their time in Washington.

The environment for public service leadership has substantially changed since the Truman Scholarship Foundation was created. Public trust in government has plummeted over the past forty-plus years, and the shift in public attitudes makes the challenges to morale for those who aspire to be leaders in public service more acute. The Summer Institute and other programming by the foundation seek to build community among scholars—within their yearly cohorts and across the forty-three classes of Trumans—in ways that mitigate the effects of this difficult environment on personal and professional goals. In fact, for many Truman Scholars, programs like the Summer Institute are more important than the scholarship money, and that makes the investment in programming worth every penny spent.

3

The Truman Scholar Community
Unconventional Scholarship Serving the Public Good

TARA YGLESIAS

One of the Truman Foundation's proudest accomplishments is its reputation for being accessible and transparent. The foundation offers a wealth of information to faculty representatives and applicants via our website, and we provide prompt and responsive answers to phone and email inquiries, giving feedback on the written applications of those candidates not selected for interview. There are very few questions, if any, that the foundation will not answer when it comes to our process and mission.

But with a full-time staff of five, a massive selection cycle, and the strikingly limited budget that can only be found at a government agency, there are a number of questions that we simply cannot answer to our satisfaction or the satisfaction of faculty representatives. Every faculty representative's favorite unanswerable Truman question is "Why wasn't my [insert superlative] student selected?"

The foundation can normally answer this question insofar as it relates to someone not selected for interview—the staff attends the entire reading panel and creates written notes about each reader. Issues with the written application are of a finite range and largely explicable. (Please see Chapter 11: "You Sank My Fellowship: The 'Near-Miss' Truman Application" for more on this topic).

Answering the question is more difficult for those students selected to interview but not selected as scholars. Foundation staff members (if one is present) attend different interviews. Since we cannot offer feedback on all interviews, we feel it would be unfair to offer feedback on some. But, even if the same foundation member were present at every interview, it might still be difficult to articulate why one student was selected over another.

At the finalist level, candidates are almost uniformly excellent. Each applicant presents a persuasive case for future leadership, provides an extensive record of public service, and offers ample evidence of academic merit. Most candidates handle the interview with aplomb, even if they believe otherwise. Selection panels are usually left with very difficult choices among candidates who are ranked very closely. Often the distinction rests on a simple, but intangible, criterion: "Will this candidate add something to the Truman Scholar community?" Since most of the panelists are Truman Scholars, the answer to this question is often based on their own experience with and perception of the Truman community. Understanding the Truman Scholar community and the value placed on it by scholars can be helpful in discerning why an applicant is or is not selected as a scholar.

The Truman Community: More than a Check

When the foundation started in the late 1970s, scholars were treated to a brief weekend in Missouri and given what, at the time, was a generous check. As the cost of education rose and additional appropriation from Congress in an amount that would substantially change the award seemed unlikely, the foundation began to examine alternative ways to add value to the program. Recognizing the importance of interpersonal connection and support, the foundation began instead to focus on better ways to develop the community of scholars.

In the early 1990s, the foundation implemented the first program to enhance the community of Truman Scholars—the Truman Scholars Leadership Week (TSLW). The program had a simple goal: bring scholars together for a week to instill in them a sense of community and underscore the value of public service, to provide information on a variety of other competitive fellowships, public service career paths, and distinguished graduate schools, and to ask scholars to work together on group policy projects and community service projects.

At first, given the diversity of student backgrounds, interests, and goals, the foundation leadership was not certain that the one-week program would be enough time to effectively build a community. As it turned out, building community was much easier than anyone anticipated. In spite of all of their differences, the scholars came together almost immediately, thanks to their shared values and newfound love of fried ravioli. Rather than dueling resumes, there were numerous conversations on how to sustain a lifetime in public service. Self-promotion turned into roommate promotion ("He did this amazing fruit bat project in Costa Rica!"). Even the competition for class speaker—such as it was—turned into a tug of war between two people who each thought the other would be the better speaker. To the foundation's surprise, scholars from different social, political, economic, and educational backgrounds easily came together to form lasting relationships.

Scholars also quickly developed relationships with the foundation staff and the Senior Scholars, distinguished Truman alumni who are invited to staff TSLW. Many Senior Scholars found future interns, staffers, and partners in advocacy in this group. "Who was your Senior Scholar?" is a favorite bonding question among many in the Truman community. Senior Scholar trading cards were clearly an overlooked revenue stream.

The Truman Community: More than a Week

Within a few years of the creation of TSLW, the foundation started the Truman Summer Institute (SI) as a way to continue the Truman community beyond the extended ice cream social that is TSLW. SI allows scholars to go to Washington, DC, the summer after they finish college to engage in a variety of foundation programming as well as a summer-long internship with a government agency or nonprofit.

Students quickly begin to build community during SI. Although most of these students have no prior relationship other than spending a week together in Missouri, they are immediately drawn to one another as old friends. Within a week, they have set up communal dinner parties, service activities, and LSAT study groups.

For many scholars, SI is where the most interesting opportunities arise. Scholars with backgrounds in science find themselves working with children—not numbers—for the first time ever. Scholars who were planning to go straight to graduate school are suddenly fielding job offers from their summer employers (and some are even more surprised to find that these employers might be willing to pay for graduate school). Scholars who never planned on entering elected office fall in love with the magic of Capitol Hill, and occasionally those who planned to run for office fall out of love with the magic of Capitol Hill.

The foundation knows that the scholars arrive with preconceived notions of DC, and it works to shatter them. The SI programming intentionally stays away from monument tours and quintessential DC experiences. The scholars have access to distinguished Truman Scholars, who visit as speakers, but the foundation often encourages conversation about the speaker's public service journey, rather than public policy debates or talking points. The program takes the scholars into neighborhoods so that they can see DC as more than just a selection of monuments. The foundation emphasizes the role the arts play in both DC culture and public policy. Most of all, the foundation offers SI participants informal opportunities to engage with the larger community of scholars in DC. Those informal meetings—potlucks, evenings at Jazz in the Garden, book talks, and afternoons on the National Mall—often provide the best community-building.

After the SI program ends, scholars have the opportunity to stay in DC for the Truman-Albright Fellows Program. This program, generously underwritten by Foundation President Madeleine Albright, assists Truman Scholars in finding year-long (or more) placements in the DC area, most with the federal government. Truman Scholars are eligible for direct appointment to federal agencies, which means the foundation is able to provide scholars a number of significant listings for entry-level employment. Most of these positions have been held by a rotating cast of Truman Scholars for many years, so agencies have come to rely on these positions for high-level, substantive work.

Scholars who participate in the Truman-Albright Fellows Program also have a number of professional development opportunities and small discussions with high-level Truman Scholars, and a small group meeting with Secretary Albright. The fellows also engage in a variety of social activities both planned by the foundation and by the fellows themselves. Election night parties are a special favorite. Each fellow is provided with a Truman Scholar mentor, who serves as an excellent resource for graduate school and career assistance. Several of these matches have turned into lifelong mentor relationships.

The Truman Community: More Than Graduate School Funding

The Truman Foundation commits significant time to surveying applicants, faculty representatives, and scholars. Nearly all of these groups agree that students are more likely to remain in public service if they receive some sort of public service inoculation, every now and again. With this in mind, the foundation created a number of shorter programs designed for those scholars who have already started graduate school.

The Public Service Law Conference (PSLC), an early program, ran in the middle 2000s with the intention of encouraging scholars in law school to stay on the path of public service. PSLC was a weekend seminar designed to provide public service guidance to those students who need it most. The conference discussed job-hunting strategies, managing debt, and avoiding burnout. Although the scholars who attended this weekend came from many different scholar years and might never have met before, the group was more cohesive than one might expect from a group of would-be lawyers. Most of the guest speakers had difficulty believing that these scholars did not all attend the same law school. The program was discontinued around the same time that many law schools began providing stronger support for public service lawyers.

The foundation then decided that it could reach a broader range of scholars through programs that focused on areas beyond law, and so came the Truman Governance Fellows Program and the Truman Democracy Fellows Program. These programs, running in alternating years, are weekend-long programs designed to bring together, across years and disciplines, groups of scholars who share common interests. Both programs take place in a workshop format, with scholars exchanging ideas and guest speakers arriving to discuss topics of general interest.

The Governance Fellows Program is designed for scholars who plan on pursuing a high-level appointment—either political or career—within the federal government. The foundation brings in a variety of scholars within the executive branch to discuss the pros and cons of government service at that level. The program also provides substantive information on how best to apply for such opportunities. The Democracy Fellows Program is designed for scholars who plan to run for public office at any level. The foundation hosts speakers with a variety of campaign experience, from school board races to the U.S. Senate. Speakers discuss useful information, such as the nuts and bolts of fundraising and phone banking, and each program cohort quickly coalesces. Though these scholars might come from many different scholar classes or varied professional experiences, and though they may hold to diverse ideologies, they are united in their desire for change.

But Wait! Isn't There More?

Whenever the foundation is asked for information about the Truman community and the opportunities it provides, invariably the names of prominent Truman Scholars come up. The foundation is proud to count among its distinguished alumni a state governor and numerous state executives. It can boast of several high-ranking government officials, judges, and legislators. The community even contains a number of media personalities and a few veterans of reality TV. One of the scholars writes romance novels when she is not serving in her state legislature. The foundation is proud of every one of these.

But we do not wish to leave the impression that such public success is all we value. One scholar is the only OB-GYN for several counties in the rural Midwest. Some scholars have founded charter schools and work every day to ensure a better education for everyone. Others are serving in the armed forces, operating research laboratories, or working at the Federal Reserve. They are professors and U.S. Attorneys and the occasional public defender. There are Truman Scholar engineers and chemists. Truman Scholars run food banks and mutual aid societies. These scholars who often labor without public recognition are as important to the foundation's mission as those who are more famous.

The foundation staff is pleased to have had a part in creating a community that values all of these people equally. We are proud that our scholars rarely let their egos get in the way of their service to others. And we are happy to welcome into the community all those who share the notion that public service is of the highest value, regardless of whether a person wants to contribute through medicine, engineering, the law, art, or public policy. President Truman would not have it any other way.

4

Public Service, Power, and the Challenges Facing Future Public Servants

ANDREW RICH

A well-functioning society requires effective public servants. They are the people who teach our children and keep our children healthy. They build our roads and our spacecraft. They protect our people and our planet. They are scientists and soldiers, social workers and city planners, grassroots activists and elected officials. They are first responders in emergencies and the last people defending our rights. Public service is tough; it is often unglamorous. But it is essential.[1]

As a society, we are off on the wrong track in so many ways in supporting and encouraging public service—on the wrong track for public servants who want to make a difference in politics and government, in particular. This has happened, especially over the past thirty-five years, in ways that smart, ambitious young people perceive. As a result, too often millennials and Gen Zers do not view public service—and especially government —as a way to make a positive difference. Too few of the best aspire to it. If we do not turn this trend around, we risk having too many of the wrong kinds of people in public service—those who misunderstand power and how to make change. Or perhaps understand it too well but do not intend to use it for purposes that improve society.

The national fellowships community provides an important line of defense against this problem. We make a difference in affecting the career paths of talented and ambitious young people. All of us have the chance to engage students at a particularly crucial moment in their professional development around questions of power, politics, service, and democracy. Doing that in ways that encourage outstanding young people to consider and see the value of careers in public service is an exciting and essential project.

Future Leaders and Public Service

By all accounts, the challenges facing our country are enormous, and by most accounts, our political institutions and leaders are ill-equipped to address them. This is not a political or ideological point. Rather, this is an observation about the weakness of our political institutions. On the one hand, most institutions were created for particular purposes in the twentieth century, and they have had difficulty adapting to the needs and concerns of the twenty-first century. On the other hand, there is an assessment of our political leaders in both parties, who too often seem polarized, incapable of action, and beholden to special interests.

The problems in our politics run deep. They took decades to create, and these are conditions that will take time for us to improve. At the end of the day, I am optimistic about what is possible, however, because I think millennials and Gen Zers have much to offer if they can figure out how to connect their ambitions to public service.

Admittedly, on first blush, current college students give us plenty of reason to worry. The complaints about their generation are well documented. They appear to have an increased sense of entitlement. They are attached—all the time—by their thumbs to their phones, and they are often not very adept at establishing real human connections. While there is evidence for these claims, when it comes to public service, they might just be our hope.

Research suggests that millennials and Gen Zers are civic-minded generations.[2] They are group-oriented, problem-solving, institution builders or, in other words, "we" generations. Students today engage in community service at much higher rates than previous generations; this is especially true for those who attend college. In 2014, 88 percent of college freshmen reported that they had participated in community service in high school, and 60 percent of those graduating from college indicated that they want to engage in service to "help the country." A Pew survey indicated then that 58 percent of millennials had "done volunteer activities through or for an organization" within the previous year and Gen Z students are on a similar path to service.[3]

So what is the problem? It has to do with how students over the last two decades have engaged civically compared with previous generations. They are not voting—at least not at the rates of previous generations when they were young. Millennials made up 19 percent of the 2012 electorate. In 2016, they represented 31 percent of the electorate—as big a part of the electorate as baby boomers. In 2016, only 50 percent of millennials voted, less than older generations.[3] The voting turnout in the 2020 election saw a marked increase in the number of millennial and Gen Z voters. While that is very encouraging, we have yet to see whether or not that will be a permanent change.

Most millennials are now working, and they want to engage in their careers in different ways. They think about power and freedom (and risk) differently from older generations. They are not attracted to working in the public service institutions—government and the nonprofit sector —that their parents and grandparents created. Many have little interest in politics, as such. Many are not particularly interested in Washington, DC. In fact, they are often distrustful of Washington. They identify less often as partisan—at least in the ways that older Americans might categorize themselves as Democrats or Republicans. They are civically minded as problem solvers, concerned with issues, and quite often, concerned either at the transnational level or at the local level.

When I was director of the Truman Scholarship Foundation, I spent the month of March on the road for Truman finalist interviews. I participated in two hundred interviews, and a career goal we heard a lot was social entrepreneurship: the desire to accomplish social goals—and make society better—through the methods of the private sector. Truman candidates see more possibility for impact through entrepreneurship than government, and they are attracted to the possibilities for immediate, measurable results that social entrepreneurship claims to provide. While perhaps fine for some, this preference misses key opportunities for millennials and Gen Zers to engage the institutions of government, in particular—where the greatest power resides and where change can be scaled for the largest numbers to benefit.

The Challenges of Public Service

So what is going on here? Evidence suggests that students in college and young professionals have sized up the world that their parents have handed them, and they are making some reasonable judgments about what is possible and where best to expend their energy. The orienting event for most young people when it comes to civic engagement is 9/11 and its aftermath. For those drawn to public service, it is a defining event, and for many it is *the* defining event from their childhood that has set the stage for so much that has come since. Millennials have grown up in the midst of two wars; during Truman interviews, I was frequently reminded that millennials cannot remember a time when the United States was not at war. In addition, they and their families experienced the deep recession of 2008—the collapse of the housing market and the financial sector. They have lived through a slow recovery, one in which they have experienced the disproportionate effects of youth unemployment, which remains in double digits at just more than 10 percent.[4]

Then, they look at government, and they see sclerosis—inaction, polarization, and corruption. Young people have a hard time naming domestic political figures whom they admire. They are distressed by the role of money in politics and the disproportionate influence of lobbyists. They do not see political institutions working effectively, and they do not see them as a way to address the problems that animate their interests in public service.

All of this is reinforced by dominant narratives in the United States that bolster a distrust of government. For many, these narratives are as influential as reality. I spent much of the early part of my career studying the "war of ideas" in American politics—the growth of a free-market, conservative movement, in particular, that succeeded at discrediting government. This movement reshaped the point of departure in public and policy discussions so that government is seldom perceived as an effective vehicle for constructive change.

In the end, young people, by and large, have not experienced government in positive ways. And they have not been witness to or participants in movements that demonstrate how government can be successful. And so young people who are civically minded are thinking about public service in different ways. The bad news—at least I fear—is that all of this drives good young people away.

Combine everything that I have just described with the well-honed systems of private sector job recruitment that exist on many campuses, and it becomes no surprise that some of the most talented young people— including those who want to make a difference—become susceptible to the relentless and sophisticated recruitment efforts of Silicon Valley, management consulting firms, and Wall Street. In 2016, applications for summer positions with Goldman Sachs from college students and recent college graduates were at record levels. Goldman Sachs received almost 250,000 applications for summer employment—a 46 percent increase over 2012.[5] These young people, at least in surveys, indicate in overwhelming numbers that they want to have careers that make a difference. But they do not see government—or even nonprofits—as the way to do it.

The Path Forward

So I worry—especially about how the current realities and perceptions of public service affect those who might aspire to it. I worry because the belief that young people can make change through the institutions of capitalism rather than democracy misunderstands some key possibilities around the effective exercise of power in our society. Fundamentally, for democracy to work, we have to engage government, including Washington, where so much power resides. We need young people to engage government. They have to understand and grapple with how change on a broad-based scale requires the power that can only be found in government. Millennials and Gen Zers certainly do not need to share a view of government's appropriate role, but they have to engage government in serious ways.

I worry, but I am optimistic. Those of us who are a little older have made something of a mess of our politics and our institutions of public service. But there is growing evidence that some portion of millennials and Gen Zers wants to fix things. They just want to do it, perhaps quite rationally, by challenging our institutions from the outside. We are knee deep in a movement for immigration reform in this country, and these generations are at the front, driving it from the outside. Millennials and Gen Zers are leaders in building movements and organizing for change on a wide range of issues and on all sides of politics. While there is growing evidence that these generations may not be immediately attracted to traditional public service institutions, they are interested in challenging the power of these institutions from the outside, from both the right and the left—and from new angles and perspectives.

The Truman Foundation aims to support this work, and all of us in the national fellowships community can encourage it among outstanding young people. The Truman Foundation is attracted to candidates who have an analysis of how power operates to scale change and progress within our society. They look for candidates who would like to use power to make change—whether by challenging systems of power from the outside or aspiring to accumulate power within institutions. Our vision is a country that deeply values the diverse and innovative ways that Americans make a positive difference in the lives of others through public service.

President Truman once defined courage as "not always facing the foe, but [. . .] taking care of those at home with a true heart and a strong mind." Today we too often think of courage in political terms and taking a stand against a party or a policy. Young people on the verge of or just now entering public service often have a different vision, and I think President Truman would approve. What is needed is more courage to take bold chances, try new things, and explore new approaches. "The buck stops here" is Truman's most famous line. It speaks to accountability and the need to see a job done, whether that was getting a road built, the military desegregated, or rebuilding postwar Europe. This is no different today, with pressing challenges ranging from crumbling infrastructure to combating climate change and terrorism. The best public servants are steadfast in their determination to make a difference through deeds not words. They must act with an understanding of and a resolve to engage power and institutions.

At the end of the day, I am cautiously optimistic that millennials and the Gen Zers who are following quickly after them might help us get to a better place in our politics. They now represent one in three voters. They are currently ambivalent about government and our political parties. But my hope—and I think there is some evidence to back this up—is that they will remake them. And they may remake our understandings of politics in the process.

Part II

Applying for the Truman Scholarship

5

Suspenders and a Belt
Overpreparation and the Overachiever

TARA YGLESIAS

Little is more prized among the Truman community than the privilege of sitting on a regional review panel. These are the panels that select Truman Scholars and thereby identify tomorrow's public service leaders. These spots are jealously guarded and turnover is infrequent. The foundation has several panelists whose service began in the 1990s. Previous executive secretary Andrew Rich, current executive secretary Terry Babcock-Lumish, and I have served on Truman panels since the early 2000s, so those of us who participate in Truman interview panels tend to take the long view of history.

We will see short trend cycles. Who does not remember when tuberculosis had a moment circa 2004 or that time jumpsuits made a mild interview fashion splash in 2015?[1] But major shifts in applications or applicants take years to emerge. Yet in the years following 2016, we reached a sudden tipping point on a trend that had been building ever since the first hand-wringing think piece on millennials hit the pages of *The Chronicle*. Our candidates were overprepared.

We have seen candidates suffering from this malady before—canned responses have been the bane of the interviewer's existence at least since someone coined the phrase "talking points," but beginning in 2016, the foundation started hearing feedback like:

- *It is as if they are accessing files of information and reading them to me.*
- *I wish they had abandoned their talking points and interacted with the panel more.*
- *They seemed unwilling to engage with the questions.*

The interviews had a bit of a surreal quality to them—we asked questions that seemed to register only slightly with the candidate and yet the candidate produced a comprehensive answer. But these interviews felt like shaking a very wordy Magic 8 Ball. The answers, while comprehensive, were often not responsive. Generally, the feedback from interview panelists is unbridled enthusiasm mixed in with pleas to allow them to award more scholarships, but when a majority of candidates failed to engage the panel, the panel's enthusiasm was much diminished.

After one early panel in 2016, the Truman team had a long discussion and came to the conclusion that part of the problem was that these students were lacking in authenticity. But it was not that they never had authenticity—it was that the authenticity had been wrung from them. After hearing one candidate describe a series of "murder boards" that seemed more vigorous than most dissertation defenses, and having no other candidate find this description at all strange, we settled upon the word "overprepared" as a fine catchall to describe what we were seeing. This word seems to encapsulate all the problems—lack of engagement, inability to stretch intellectually, lack of displayed passion or authenticity—but it also acknowledged that students were taking this seriously.

The foundation was still selecting the same scholars that we would have otherwise—and not every student who came before the panelists could be categorized as overprepared. But for a good portion, if not an outright majority, their earnest preparation now threatened to be their undoing. Panelists noticed this issue across gender presentation, institution, and geography. Preparation is intended to make the interview experience better, but for the overprepared student, the opportunity to test their mettle was likely unsatisfying. Once students have had eleven practice interviews, they really have seen it all. But in an effort to improve things for those who remained to be interviewed, I dashed off an email to the NAFA listserv, started warning candidates not to be too reliant on practice sessions, and we rode out the rest of the cycle.

But then overprepared began to have a moment.

How Is It Possible to Overprepare?

After the 2016 presidential debates, MSNBC's Chuck Todd criticized Hillary Clinton for being overprepared.[2] Discussions unfolded about whether it is even possible to overprepare and, assuming it is, whether overpreparedness is worthy of criticism. Attempts were made to justify and explain the term as a substitute for everything from clarity of expression to authenticity of delivery. The concept of overpreparation as a criticism was derided as a gendered insult—a way to communicate that a woman was demonstrating unseemly ambition or was being more intellectual than acceptable.

Which left me with the earlier assessment of overprepared Truman candidates and how strange it was to be talking about students being too prepared. Were we criticizing them for taking this too seriously? Was "overprepared" a code word for something else? Had a scholarship that often rewards the wonky just turned on the wonks?

Absent perhaps assuming leadership of an entire country, most human endeavor has a point at which preparation has diminishing returns. Studying into the wee hours versus getting a decent night's sleep, for instance. At some point after diminishing returns, preparation begins to turn on the diligent. That is when, for example, the overplanned family vacation turns into a bleak hellscape.[3]

But in these instances neither the diligent student nor National Lampoon's Clark Griswold can be fairly criticized for overpreparing—and the same is true of Truman candidates. These students are taking the process seriously and investing time and effort into being successful. Taking the process seriously is not worthy of criticism, but it is subject to critique.

Sounds Like Someone's Got a Case of the "Overs"

The foundation's critique began with looking at our panels and honestly evaluating the feedback we were getting to see if we were using "overprepared" as a code word for something else. The first concern, in light of the criticism swirling around the word as a gendered insult, was to see to whom this term applied.

Overpreparedness was ecumenical in a lot of ways: the foundation received feedback from every panel; the issue was not specific to particular schools; and a representative number of students across gender presentations was affected.[4] There was some variation in how overpreparation manifested itself. Some candidates were anxious, others glib. Panelists saw those with polished scripts and those unable to utter complete sentences. There were interviews where candidates seemed wholly inauthentic, and then others where candidates were so agitated that their entire psyche appeared on display. Even with this constellation of symptoms, the panelists were certain that overpreparation was the culprit because all of these candidates had a few things in common:

- *They were overscripted.* All candidates should have a certain set of points that they wish to cover during the interview. It is acceptable to consider responses to frequently asked interview questions. But there is a point after which we descend into madness. No matter the nuance of the question, the candidate is going to shoehorn in that response everyone on Practice Interview #12 enjoyed so much. Instead of a flowing conversation, the interview feels as if the candidate is trying to recite a long-form poem but keeps getting interrupted with unrelated questions.[5] Candidates may artfully arrange not only their responses, but also their casual interactions with the panel.[6] Occasionally, panelists come across a candidate who has scripted their entire persona, focusing on the Truman not out of a genuine interest in public service, but out of an attempt to seek accolades. Both the robotic know-it-all (entirely scripted answers) and the odious toady (entirely scripted persona) were criticized by panelists for a lack of authenticity. This lack of authenticity leads to an unsatisfying interview for all concerned.
- *They are overwrought.* Nerves are perfectly normal and should vary by candidate. But over the past several years, candidates have become increasingly overwrought at all aspects of the interview process. What used to be a charming amount of second guessing about their answers has morphed into a postmortem that is simultaneous

with the interview itself. Panelists are seeing more candidates who freeze during the interview or burst into tears during or immediately after. We often see them slumped on a cell phone in the hallway vividly recreating the interview for their trusted confidant with purple prose and dizzying inaccuracy. The overwrought candidate may take every question as a personal affront, unable to engage in the sort of intellectual exercise that is a necessary part of a thorough interview. Others carry the burdens of the hopes of others into the interview; while these burdens can be helpful and informative of a candidate's motivations, such pressure can also be the undoing of a candidate.

- *They are overwhelmed.* Interviews are complicated and mystical things, so it is only natural for candidates to feel a bit overwhelmed. Candidates are presented with a huge volume of information—from our website, from their school, from former Truman Scholars—and have no understanding of how to synthesize any of it. I have promised myself not to engage in Gen Z bashing, but this generation of candidates is both unused to failure and more anxious overall.[7] These are the candidates for whom practice interviews ratchet up stress levels because that experience suggests to them that there is a right answer if they just look hard enough. After every question, interviewers watch as they try to synthesize various contradictory bits of feedback into a unified whole—thus they will be authentic and measured, passionate and pragmatic, chatty and formal all at the same time. The overwhelmed candidate can have the least satisfying experience of all. Often they spend more effort on the Sisyphean task of figuring out the right answer than allowing the panel to get to know them.

You Promised No Gen Z Bashing, but . . .

Overprepared students are nothing new to the world of competitive scholarships. On some level, the Truman stock in trade is the kid who always has time to make another set of flashcards, read another article, and set up another informational interview. But we have quickly gone from the charmingly wonky candidate who tries to insert a Harry Truman reference just to show he made it through David McCullough's doorstop of a biography, to hordes of simulacra of this candidate, entirely without the charm. But the interesting part is that the candidates do have the charm and personality needed to have a good interview experience, but they cannot manage to show the interviewers what their recommendation writers see.

In many ways, Gen Z students, like millennials before them, are uniquely prone to the downsides of overpreparation. First, like millennials, Gen Z students report more stress than other generations.[8] They are naturally going to fall into the "overwhelmed" category and stay there. Panelists do not expect students to enter the interview stress-free. Indeed, my recollection of my own blasé Generation X–style interview suggests that we do not want to return to the dystopian past either. But candidates need to be able to manage their stress levels in the lead up to the interview so that they can engage the panel without resorting to either dry recitation or unhinged spectacle.

Second, Gen Z applicants (like millennials before them) tend to function more collaboratively than previous generations. We see the change in their applications. Gone are the days of campus dictators; we are in the era of leadership councils and copresidents. Setting aside the issues that this collaboration presents when trying to suss out whether a candidate is a leader and change agent, the collaboration leads to the unintended consequence of creating a stress echo chamber. Everyone on leadership council is invested in the candidate, and they are all stressed out. Well-meaning friends and mentors try to help in ways that only exacerbate the problem. Then the pressure to keep up with friends ("She did seven practice interviews, and I have only done six!") can undo any effort at moderation and appropriate preparation.

Finally, and speaking of keeping up with friends, the Internet certainly plays a role in the overpreparation of these students. In the dark ages, pre–dial-up candidates were limited in the information to which they had access. Schools could provide contacts and advice, there were probably some physical books at the library, and the truly ambitious would find an actual phone book and reach out to past candidates and recipients of an award. But today, candidates are able to reach out to any past candidate or recipient through a click of a mouse. While this development is generally positive and has opened the competition to candidates from a wide array of institutions, such ease of access also complicates things. Candidates begin to compare themselves—favorably or not—to profiles they read on the Internet. They reach out to candidates and winners, taking their advice, no matter how contradictory or inapplicable, and try to apply it to their own candidacy. When they have exhausted those routes, candidates venture down the dark path of random googling, finding all manner of inaccurate advice and attempting to synthesize it with all the other pieces of advice that they have received. Then candidates reflexively check in on social media to see how many of their friends had practice interviews that day. These tendencies result in a toxic slurry that can undo any candidate not able to properly evaluate the advice they are receiving.

I've Unplugged the Internet; What Else Should I Do?

At the outset, those invested in this process should recognize that the best Truman candidates are the overachievers, and there is almost nothing one can do to stop an overachiever from attempting to overachieve. These candidates will, regardless of instruction, worry and do and think too much about their interview. If these candidates are using preparation as armor, the goal of the advisor is to keep them from adding so much protection that they can never walk into battle.

Advisors should begin by having an honest conversation about the level of preparation they recommend. This comment assumes that the advisor has begun to *really* think about this question as well. It is imperative that advisors spend some time thinking about the value of different types of preparation. The foundation recognizes that some of these items are outside of the advisor's control. Some will likely not get away with giving one student four practice sessions and another two, even if that makes the most sense for the candidate. But advisors can make the practice sessions more or less formal, depending on the candidate. Consider what is driving certain exercises. Will they be beneficial for the student? Or are they practices that should be abandoned?[9]

After reviewing both the foundation's and the student's materials, the advisor should have a frank discussion with the candidate about the type of preparation that is recommended and the type that is not.[10] This information should be moderated depending on the candidate. But at a minimum, candidates need to be told how to sift through the advice they are receiving. Not all well-meaning advice needs to be followed. People tend to give advice from their own personal interests and shortcomings, so candidates should keep that in mind when deciding which information to rely upon. While the process changes little from year to year, current information is generally more reliable than even the most persuasive alumnus Truman Scholar. And, above all, keep in mind that the foundation has never told anyone why they were selected.[11] Beware of anyone claiming to have the answer to the question of how one gets selected to be a Truman Scholar.

Which brings me to the most sensitive topic for any NAFA member: the answers and who has them. Some questions have answers (what are your stated criteria?) and others do not (how do those criteria get applied over a variety of factors that we cannot possibly know or control for?). How much preparation is needed to become a Truman Scholar is one of those questions without an answer. Or, to be fair, without an answer that either the foundation or advisors would want to share with people. Because there is no amount of preparation that will make someone a Truman Scholar. There is the amount of preparation needed to allow candidates to be authentic and as comfortable as possible, but that only allows them to have a valuable interview experience; it does not guarantee success.

But if advisors focus on the value of the process, they can offer all candidates a valuable and useful experience. After providing sound and persuasive advice about the need to stay off Google and the inappropriateness of canned response flashcards, advisors will find that candidates will do these things anyway. Most candidates are able to recite all the questions they were asked in their practice interview.[12] All of them. The only result of such an exercise is that they can then answer any question—but only the way it was posed to them during their mock interview. At that point, advisors need to shake up the process in order to get any positive results. One way to do that is by altering the type of questions asked during practice interviews. Committee members need to take specific policy positions they might not otherwise take and argue from those positions. Advisors should bring in real-world practitioners to ask questions from procedural and grassroots perspectives as well as questions outside the candidate's field.[13] Even something as simple as moving to a different location for an interview or asking the candidate to wear a suit can help them to engage rather than go on performance autopilot.

Affirmatively encourage candidates to stay out of the dark corners of the Internet. If they must google, have them google news articles related to their topic of interest. It is of course possible for that to go wrong as well, but then the interview is back into charming wonk territory and that is fine with panelists. Tell them to be judicious about who they reach out to for advice and how to apply it to their own situations. Remind them of the uniqueness of the interview process—what worked for one person in one situation is not likely to work again, simply because that interview will never be conducted the same way twice.

Each application and each applicant is distinct—the point of the interview is to try to understand those distinctions and see how well they match up with the goals of our program. For the foundation, a successful process is one in which we are able to find those candidates who best match our goals, while providing a valuable experience for those candidates who are not selected. Candidates who present themselves authentically, even if that means they are less than perfect, stand a much better chance of not only being selected as a Truman Scholar, but also finding the process valuable when they are not selected. Advisors should encourage candidates to underprepare a bit—just this once—to have a much more worthwhile interview experience.

6

Non Ducor, Duco
Leadership and the Truman Scholarship Application[1]

TARA YGLESIAS

Leadership is one of the core components of any successful scholarship application. Whether students are interested in the arts, government service, medicine, or academic research, students must be able to demonstrate that they will be agents for change in a chosen discipline. This quality is what essentially convinces the committee that the student is a good investment—and that providing support to the student now will likely yield returns in the future.[2]

The Truman Scholarship lists leadership, along with a commitment to public service and intellectual achievement, as one of three main criteria for selection. It is often easy for a student to identify and explain public service involvement. Providing information on intellectual achievement is also fairly straightforward. But explaining leadership is somewhat more elusive.

The Problem

Each year, the Truman Foundation offers faculty representatives feedback on the applications of those students not selected for interview. We provide this feedback in an effort to improve the applications that we receive.

↳ Q.) what has been said about
MIT Applicants?

If each faculty representative is better equipped to understand the selection criteria, then these representatives will be better able to identify and assist appropriate applicants. We believe that the feedback process can also help to level the playing field for those faculty representatives who are either new to the process or unable to dedicate as much of their time to advising as they would prefer.

But feedback has another, more mundane, purpose. Feedback is the easiest way for the foundation to determine whether its message is clear. If we see a persistent problem, we refine materials or better define terms for applicants and faculty representatives.

In a typical year, the foundation receives feedback requests on approximately a third of its files.[3] The foundation reviews the files and then provides either written or verbal feedback to the faculty representative. There is often a dialogue between the foundation and the faculty representative as points are clarified and questions asked.

The foundation also makes a point of reviewing reader comments on approximately one hundred and fifty files a year. The foundation conducts this review to ensure that readers are rating applications appropriately. We also review the comments to ensure that we provide adequate training to the readers.

Those applicants for whom faculty representatives request an appeal are also reviewed. Faculty representatives can request an appeal on any student who is not selected for an interview. These applications are closely read, along with all reader comments. The foundation receives approximately one hundred and fifty to two hundred requests for appeal each year.

There is some overlap between these groups of files, but the foundation reviews approximately one-half of unsuccessful files each year.[4] The overwhelming number of these files—approximately 85 percent— failed to advance to finalist status in part because of a lack of demonstrated leadership.

For the foundation, it is nearly impossible to determine whether this failure to advance resulted from an actual lack of leadership or an inability to articulate leadership on the application. A look at how the Truman Foundation evaluates leadership may provide guidance for advisors as they assist applicants. An examination of prototypical responses to the leadership question may provide insight into the problems students face in articulating their exceptional contributions.

A Few Ground Rules

The guidelines outlined in this chapter apply only to the Truman Scholarship application process. There may be some nuggets of general applicability, but most of the comments presented here are tailored to this process. The foundation is not responsible for the application of this material in untested scholarship settings.

Additionally, I do not mean to overemphasize the role of leadership in the Truman application process. Leadership is a major component of the Truman Scholarship, but it is not the only component of a successful application. Students with unusual or modest records of leadership can sometimes be successful in the Truman application process. Similarly, students with very impressive records of leadership—but more modest records of public service—are sometimes unsuccessful in the Truman application process.

Leadership on the Truman Application

The Truman application requests a short essay on an example of leadership (Question 7), a letter of recommendation corroborating the student's leadership example, and a list of leadership roles within campus and public service activities (Questions 2 through 4—see the appendices in this volume to review the questions in the application).[5] The Institutional Nomination Letter should also address the leadership abilities of the student, but in more general terms than the letter dedicated to this issue. Students can receive up to three points for their leadership record.

The readers review the application in the order presented in the online application process: Institutional Nomination Letter, student application, policy proposal, transcript, and letters of recommendation. The most critical part of the application—as it relates to the evaluation of a student's leadership—is the response to Question 7 contained in the application itself.

The first discussion of the student's leadership occurs in the nomination letter. Readers expect this letter to be fairly general—it is meant to serve as an introduction to the application—but they do expect to get a sense of the student's overall leadership abilities and potential. Successful nomination letters paint a picture of the rest of the application. For those applicants who have either nontraditional or modest leadership records, their faculty representatives should alert readers to this issue in the letter. This letter will provide an opportunity for the faculty representative to strengthen the cases students make in their applications.

The letter of recommendation on leadership should confirm the activity that the student chooses to write about in Question 7. The author need not be witness to the entire event; they only need to be comfortable confirming the essential details. The most helpful letters explain the student's leadership style, putting achievements in context. This letter can often provide details and relationships that the student will not have the opportunity to discuss in the response to Question 7.

The application asks for leadership roles in response to Questions 2 through 4.[6] Successful responses to these questions show an applicant who is progressively increasing responsibility and involvement in activities that are important to the applicant. However, students often make the mistake of assuming that readers are familiar with every campus activity and every community organization. Successful applicants tend to offer specific information about their activities so readers can better understand both the activity and the student's role in the activity.

Most students have difficulty with the essay—and the essay is the most vital part of the leadership assessment. The essay is where students articulate their leadership style. It is through this lens that the readers try to determine whether these leadership skills are likely to make the student a future agent for change.

Less-Than-Helpful Leadership Responses

Although readers see a number of ineffective leadership responses, these responses tend to fall into one of five categories.

1. *"I did a great job!"* This essay usually involves students performing a task that is part of an internship or other activity. The task is generally solitary—organizing an event or revamping a process—and much of the essay is spent explaining the various challenges encountered. The difficulty with responses like this is that students never really display leadership; they only display competence.

2. *"It rubbed off on me!"* This essay generally describes a compelling

example of another student's leadership. The student often follows an actual leader, generally in an elected office, and spends much of the essay explaining how the applicant continued in the footsteps of this other, likely superior, student. This essay fails to articulate the leadership style of the applicant, serving only as confirmation that the student knows good leadership when they see it.

3. *"I never met an office I didn't like!"* These applicants often have many leadership titles peppered throughout their applications, but are not actual leaders. The telltale sign is that students will be unable to cite a *single* compelling example of leadership in their essays. The student will try to work in multiple roles and examples to pad what is essentially the essay of an office placeholder. The problem with these applicants is that they often confuse titles with leadership. Simply occupying an office does not make the student a leader.

4. *"I lead . . . by example!"* This essay is usually seen in an application where there is a lot of public service but very little leadership. Students will often resort to explaining how they had an impact on an issue by doing something—generally solitary, but sincere nonetheless—not leading anyone. These essays not only fail to explain how the student can be a leader, but they also tend to be a red flag that leadership abilities of the applicant are rather thin.

5. *"There's no 'I' in team!"* This essay generally follows the exploits of a committee-led organization, a team of copresidents, or a group of students. Although there may be individual leadership, the essay generally masks this by focusing on the activities of the group rather than the activities of the applicant. This essay often reflects the sincere belief that the applicant did not accomplish anything alone. But readers tend to find these essays unhelpful. They know that the student appreciates the input of others, but would much rather be presented with a clear picture of the student's leadership abilities.

Helpful Leadership Responses

We see a variety of leadership roles assumed by successful Truman applicants. Some students may occupy traditional leadership roles on campus. Others may lead a grassroots movement. Still others are leaders in research or in the laboratory. Although the topics of these essays might be divergent, all of them tend to have the following elements:

1. *Identifies a significant problem.* Leadership examples are most compelling when the student writes about an issue that the student feels is important. The passion shown toward the issue not only comes out in the written application, but also in the interview. An essay on a matter to which students are willing to dedicate a professional career is always more compelling than a piece on the importance of a balanced student government budget.

2. *Defined and unique role.* Simply put, the essay should be one that could only be written by the student. If the school has, for example, twenty student senators—and each one of them could produce a similar essay—the student should probably explore other options. Successful essays not only make the role of the student quite clear but also show how the student was the only person who could have fulfilled this leadership role.

3. *Participation of others.* In order for readers to assess the leadership of applicants, students need to interact with others and explain how this interaction is a by-product of their leadership. Successful essays acknowledge the contributions of others and also show how the leader was able to utilize those contributions.

4. *Concrete outcome.* Successful essays tend to point to some concrete outcome as the result of the student's involvement. The scope of this outcome is somewhat immaterial, but the outcome should be defined and quantifiable. Students should avoid generalities such as "increased awareness" or "involved new students in the issue" unless these items can be quantified.

5. *Recent.* The readers are most interested in seeing applicants who are getting more responsible and more involved with each passing year. The idea is that scholars will be tremendous future leaders, not that they peaked in high school.

Articulating Leadership

Even with these guidelines, some students will still have a difficult time drafting a successful leadership essay. A few of these students might not have the necessary leadership abilities to produce successful applications. But the majority of students do. It may just take a bit of work to have the student seize upon the right leadership example. Some things to consider:

1. *Thinking too narrowly.* Students often equate leadership with an established title. Although students who occupy these offices can be leaders, they can also be mere holders of a title who demonstrate no leadership skills. Some of the most compelling leadership essays are written about a time when a student sees a problem and steps in with a solution. Although the student did not have a title on which to base this authority, the student is recognized as an authority. Encourage students to think broadly about leadership and consider writing the essay about something other than occupying an office. The essay is really the only place on the application to articulate a nontraditional example of leadership; the students should take advantage of this opportunity.

2. *Confusing change agent with facilitator.* Although nontraditional examples of leadership are fine, students should take care not to conflate leadership with organization. Frequently, students will assume that providing a service, such as organizing an event or facilitating a heated discussion, is always an example of leadership. Although these activities can have elements of leadership, students should be able to point to a way in which they *transformed* the process rather than just helped it along.

3. *Toot! Toot!* Many of the best Truman candidates are those students who are averse to blowing their own horn. These students spend a great deal of time thinking about others, and very little appreciating their own achievements. Although this quality is admirable, it tends to lead to essays that spend more time discussing the contributions of others or downplaying the role of the student. Some ground can be gained in the supporting letters, but it is much more interesting to the readers if students can process their own leadership experience. These students will often need to be pushed to discuss

their achievements. Question 7 is the *I/me* question of the application; readers are not interested in seeing the pronoun *we* in this essay. Question 8, on the other hand, is the place where the readers expect to see very little *I/me* and a lot of *we/they*.[7]

4. *Leading by Committee.* The problem of modesty is somewhat complicated by a few of the more interesting elements of recent generations. Many of these students think that leadership is a four-letter word. They take a dim view of students who are overly involved or who enjoy being singled out. Although all young people display a natural distrust of authority, this generation tends to reject both the authority figures as well as the systems. As a result, students often do not take advantage of leadership opportunities that are part of a recognized system. These students also tend to be very collaborative. They seek support from others and like to rule by consensus. Collaborative leadership that displays a distrust of authority can be translated into a successful Truman application, but students must recognize that their essay must appeal to a broad range of readers, including a few who come from generations that actually liked (or currently occupy) authority.

Articulating leadership in the Truman application is no easy task. Identifying an example of leadership will be difficult for many Truman applicants. These students tend to think of others before thinking of themselves. Expressing this leadership example is even more complicated. We ask students to be unique, relevant, and concrete in 2,000 characters or less. Perhaps the easiest thing is to define leadership itself. For that we turn to a word from our sponsor:

> *"A great leader is a man who has the ability to get other people to do what they don't want to do . . . and like it."*
>
> Harry S. Truman

7

I Love It When a Grad Plan Comes Together
Graduate School Advising and the Truman Application

TARA YGLESIAS

The Truman Scholarship staff spends a great deal of time trying to temper some of the unnecessary anxiety that surrounds the Truman application: The policy proposal, no matter how ridiculous, will cause problems only during the interview, and even then, it is unlikely to be fatal. The resource section, no matter whether a student decides on APA or MLA, will be given only a brief glance by a reader who is just trying to be sure the student looked at the right sources (and, quiet as it is kept, the reader may not even know the difference between APA and MLA). The Summer Institute question, no matter how forcefully the student answers "No!" will never derail an application. But of the remaining unloved and overlooked questions on the application, Question 11—where students describe their graduate programs—is the one that can play a critical role in both the success of the process on college campuses and the success of the application under review by the Truman selection committee.[1]

This essay will cover graduate school advising for the Truman application, tips for advising, guidance on how the readers view this section of the application, and suggestions for the writing process. As ever, while some of these bits of wisdom may be applicable to a variety of applications, my expertise lies with the Truman Scholarship program. Advisors and students should apply these suggestions to other scholarships at their peril.

Advising: So Whaddaya Wanna Do with Your Life?

My extensive knowledge of how to advise students for graduate school comes from that one time I was a student who then applied for graduate school. As a first-generation college student, step one required someone to explain to me what graduate school was—I was a bit fuzzy on that point. But other than that confusion, I was every bit as obstinate and overconfident as I am today. Advising me was likely a nightmare. There was certainly a lot of skulking and eye rolling. But I did get advice—some good, some bad, all brief—which I then applied in haphazard ways to my Truman application. I wrote a tight, focused essay on attending law school with an emphasis on clinical experience.[2] But there were no soul-searching talks over international coffee, no sudden realizations, and certainly no *feelings* of any kind. After my selection, when I was asked to speak with and mentor other Truman and Truman-like students, I could not figure out why so many wanted to talk so much about their hopes and dreams. I certainly could not imagine why someone would do such a thing with a professor, of all people. As it turned out, I was as much of a nightmare as an advisor as I was as an advisee. In short, there are professional graduate school advisors out there, perhaps reading this very sentence, who are eminently more qualified than I am to suggest how to advise students on graduate school selection.

But in my capacity at the Truman Foundation, I have vast and intensive experience cleaning up the mess made by unsuccessful graduate school advising.[3] Sometimes the problems in advising are evident in the application process. Foundation readers see essays that are unformed or ill informed. Foundation panelists have interviews with students who seem unaware of the ramifications of their graduate school plans. But for scholars, these issues can spill over into their interaction with the foundation. The foundation requires graduate school proposals before we provide funding for scholars.[4] During this process, it becomes quite obvious who either did not receive or was not amenable to graduate school advising. But the profound difference here is that we will not cut a check to a student who is unable to provide a coherent graduate school plan.

But of all the fallout from unsuccessful graduate school advising, the worst may be the scholar with *graduate school regret*. We see them, ghostly shades wandering around our offices moaning, "Why didn't anyone tell me law school is so boring?" "Everyone in my PhD program is petty and vengeful!" "No one at my [research UK masters program] even cares if I do the reading!" It can be gratifying to hear scholars say, "You told me not to do X, I did it. Now I'm miserable."

While a few of these students are the sort for whom no prior intervention would do any good, it does appear that some of these issues are preventable through the judicious dispensing of graduate school advice throughout the application process. The added benefit of providing this advice is that the graduate school portion of the Truman application process is the most portable of essays. No one may ever ask for two short sentences about the three most significant courses the student has taken, but the student can certainly reapply the information gathered in Question 11 to future graduate school essays. Of all the feedback that we get from finalists, the majority of students mention how much the discussions about graduate school helped to clarify their goals.

To that end, here are a few suggestions about on-campus advising for graduate school:[5]

- *Talk early.* Whether the advising comes from the fellowships office or elsewhere on campus, early exposure to graduate school programs and the requirements thereof is critical to future Truman (and life) success. This advice is particularly true for first-generation students, who may not be aware of the need to preplan testing and course work to meet graduate school deadlines. Early advising will also help to get those students for whom graduate school is a vague and distant idea thinking about the Truman process. Students interested in advocacy—a prime breeding ground for Truman Scholars—often spend so much time in the early years of campus life chained to a fence in protest that they never even consider graduate school. The foundation tends to run into these students much later in their careers—after they have worked for a while and now are working on the JD, MA, or PhD—and are left wondering whether they would have been outstanding Truman applicants if graduate school had appeared on the radar earlier.[6]

- *Talk often.* Students may enter an undergraduate program set on one idea (med school or bust) and cling to that idea no matter how their interests (policy wonkery is pretty cool) or abilities (Organic Chem: C-) evolve. Few young people have the ability to be self-reflective, so occasional "graduate school checkups" may be advisable. The foundation receives several applications a cycle where a student has had a clear pivot in direction; frequent advising check-ins could make this transition smoother both for the student and the application.

- *Talk only to the student.* One of the most difficult situations arises when students' ideas are not their own. Pressures from family, pro-fessors, and even advisors can overshadow a student's own interests. This situation often comes wrapped in many complex emotional and cultural factors as well—making for a thorny problem when it comes to advising. Working with students so that they can express their own ideas and needs serves them best in the long run, but it is not always easy. One of the tricks is to get students to visualize—really visualize—their lives at forty. Once advisors explain that forty will not come with Geritol and a hip replacement, scholars can understand the importance of being where they—and not their parents—want them to be. The conversation that the student needs to have with the interloper—be it a family or faculty member—may be difficult, but allowing students to express themselves authentically in their application is well worth the trouble.

- *Talk clearly.* Most students have some idea what they want to be when they grow up. The problem is that they have no idea how to get there. Starting with the dream job gives the student a concrete way to talk about what they want to do. From there, informational inter-views can be a great way to get students to understand the next steps in the process and the graduate school options available to them.

- *Talk actual as well as intellectual.* Students often get caught up in the intellectual life of graduate school. While the rigor and content of programs are important, students should also have the opportunity to explore some of the more mundane issues of graduate educa-tion. Understanding the fundamental differences between the life of a graduate student and the life of an undergraduate student is important. The foundation sees many students who imagine graduate school is just one halcyon continuation of their undergraduate career. We all know this perception to be inaccurate—we should warn students that undergraduate hijinks are not appreciated in graduate school.

- *Talk to people other than professors.* There are people in the world who are useful and happy who do not have PhDs. For many students, however, PhDs are the only people from whom they seek graduate advice. Students should speak with at least two or three people who have, fairly recently, attended programs of interest to the student. For students at campuses with graduate schools, help arrange a time for them to talk to current graduate students interested in similar issues.

- *Talk in ways that are not overly proscriptive.* Sometimes, advising is just too easy: *I want revenge on those who wronged me!* Go to law school. *I want to learn more and more about less and less.* Consider a PhD. *I enjoy playing God and am good at organic chem.* Here's a med school brochure. But without pushing at these ideas, students will never be in a position to really explain why they want these degrees. They will also not be able to defend these ideas against a harsh and unjust panel of dream-crushers (the Truman interview panel) who want to do nothing more than throw every graduate school plan into the fire and dance around the embers (or so it sometimes seems to students who have not thought through their plans).[7]

- *A few things to remember.* The Truman is unique in that the foundation allows students to take four years of deferral from the date that they complete their undergraduate education. In fact, we strongly encourage all students to take at least a year between undergraduate and graduate school. When advising students, be sure they are aware of this practice. For some, this information will reduce the pressure that they are feeling to figure out graduate school in this instant. Additionally, we do support study overseas if a student is interested in obtaining a degree from an international program.

Reading the Application: They Kill Dreams, Don't They?

Truman applications are evaluated on three main criteria: leadership, commitment to a career in public service, and likelihood of academic success in graduate school. Question 11 falls squarely within the third sphere, but its role in the application can have a direct impact on how the readers evaluate the other two.

The Nominee Rating Form includes Question 11 as part of the "appropriateness for proposed graduate study" category, along with the student's transcript, Questions 3, 6, 10, 11, 12, 13, Institution Nomination Letter, Continuing Academic Success Letter, and the policy proposal.[8] This section considers activities, grades, strength/depth and breadth of studies, quality of policy proposal, appropriateness of graduate study plans, and likely appeal to institutions listed in Question 11. But while Question 11 is one of many items considered in this category, both its location in the application and content make it an important tool for reviewers in evaluating an application.

The role of Question 11 relates to the way readers are taught to read applications.[9] Truman applications are not simply read and ranked one against the other. Readers do not tally up public service commitments and leadership positions and select the applications with the most. We read the applications in search of change agents—and what a change agent looks like depends on an area of interest, individual circumstances, and even geographic location. That variation requires readers to be flexible in their evaluation. A student who plans to have a global impact on a matter of public health will look very different from the student who plans to run for a leadership position in tribal government. The student wanting to emphasize the need for arts education will not share a lot of characteristics with the student who plans to create a fully realized neuron on a computer. Truman encourages its readers to recognize these differences. Rather than engaging in open combat to see which student has the most peer-reviewed articles published, readers just try to determine whether students have fully realized their potential to be change agents.

To do this type of evaluation, readers spend the bulk of the application review time gathering information. All through the nomination letter and Questions 1 through 8 and Question 10, readers are simply absorbing data. Question 9 is the first time a student has to present something other than a list of accomplishments. Question 9 is the amuse-bouche, in some ways—it *prepares* readers for what they are to see later in the application—but can be satisfying in its own right. Extending the metaphor, Question

11 then becomes a hearty appetizer for the main course of Questions 12 and 13.[10]

Arriving at Question 11, readers suddenly have a way to evaluate all the data they have been gathering. Does this student have the leadership, service commitment, and intellect necessary to succeed in this program? Has the student demonstrated a steadily increasing level of engagement? Do students seem to have an understanding of how to make the changes that they seek to make?

While Question 11, on its face, provides information about graduate school, the subtext of this question is very important. Students need to demonstrate an understanding of how to tackle the problems they have identified. That understanding begins (and sometimes tragically ends) with an identification of what graduate school program will best prepare them for a career in public service.

The first threshold our readers look for is whether the graduate school plans make sense for students and for issues. The sense-making threshold is often fairly low, but some students still fail to meet it. The most common issues are the following:

- *Graduate school plans that are unfocused.* Applicants still sometimes include responses that do not have degree programs listed. Others will give a general response about the importance of graduate school generally but fail to discuss any particulars.
- *Graduate school plans that are too inclusive.* Students sometimes propose unwieldy joint degrees that are essentially PhD/JD/MBAs. Whether this is hubris or uncertainty is unclear, but the response is problematic.
- *Graduate school plans that emerge from nowhere.* There should be some correlation between the student's activities, interests, and graduate program. If the response to Question 11 is a surprise, the readers will not be pleased.

Once the threshold is met, readers then begin to evaluate the response in more detail. For the purposes of this essay, these steps appear to be discrete. In reality, this evaluation takes place quickly and in no particular order. Readers look to see whether students have identified the best degree program to work on their particular issue. This determination is, of course, a bit subjective. One reader may feel strongly that a policy degree is the best choice for a student, while another may think a PhD is more appropriate. But it is important that students make their decision process explicit in the essay so the readers can follow the rationale. "Showing their work" can also help if students are selected for interview, as it will reassure panelists that selected finalists did not arrive at their degree programs lightly.

From there, the readers will look to see if the student identified the best institution for the selected degree. This determination can take into account institution specialties, the student's strengths, and institutional prestige. Readers look for specific information about institutional offerings to see whether the student has reviewed the program thoroughly. We use these distinctions to set programs apart. The readers look to see whether the student has the appropriate course work and interests for individual institutions. Institutional prestige can also be an important factor. Readers do not make direct comparisons on degree programs, so a student who proposes the number one urban planning degree in the country will not be given a higher score than the student who proposes the number 653 urban planning degree in the country. But students whose career paths are dependent on attending a prestigious program had best select graduate institutions accordingly. Conversely, readers recognize also that some students have criteria other than prestige (family commitments, geographical, or financial constraints) at play when selecting a graduate school.

A full one-third of Truman reading panels are graduate school admissions personnel or individuals who have been involved with the accreditation process for specific types of graduate schools. The remaining members of the reading panel are Truman Scholars who have attended the graduate school programs most sought after by Truman applicants. Their level of knowledge is extensive and detailed. They are quickly able to discern which students have done their homework and which have not.

The final factor is to determine whether the stated degree and program make sense for the student. While an applicant may have identified the premier doctoral program for international relations and deftly explained why such a credential would allow work on issues of human trafficking in Asia, the applicant must still make the case that the degree is appropriate. Readers look to the data they have gathered from the rest of the application to determine whether the student's abilities are likely to be a good fit for the program.

But that is not to say that the foundation has never selected applicants with poor Question 11 responses. Truman's readers and panelists all know that graduate school advising is part of the Truman process. If an applicant has a poor answer to Question 11 but otherwise possesses the qualities of a Truman Scholar, the readers or panelists will forgive the applicant. But a failure in Question 11 means that other parts of the application will need to work much harder to overcome the deficit. In an interview, a poor Question 11 can mean the student spends precious interview time defending a decision to go or not to go to law school.

Writing the Application: Advice for Advisors and Students

Much ink has been spilled over the issue of advisors and their role in the editing process. The Truman Foundation thinks it is not appropriate for advisors to do hard edits on applications. But asking questions, providing feedback, and offering students ways to improve their writing are all appropriate. For the application, Question 11 is probably the place where advisor feedback is most welcomed and expected. Advisors do not know more about their students' leadership experiences than their students do, but advisors almost certainly know more about graduate school. In most cases, advisors have attended/worked at/parked near/taught in a graduate school for more years than the students have been alive. It is absolutely appropriate to give feedback on these essays both in terms of content (directing students to investigate other programs and degrees where appropriate) and style (assisting students with expressing these ideas more effectively). If a student writes, "I plan to get a PhD in anthropology because such a credential will ensure that I receive respect and deference from my colleagues," then once the advisor has stopped laughing and wiped away the tears, it is appropriate to discuss where the student obtained the information and how this information might be perceived in an interview context (hint: also with laughter).

In terms of content, the most common mistakes are these:

• Overcredentialing: *"After obtaining my JD and PhD, I will begin my career as a program analyst at the Department of Justice."* Students seem to believe that the way to prove to us that they are smart is by obtaining a complete assortment of letters after their name.

There are very, very few people for whom such an ambitious graduate school plan makes sense. Presenting the Whitman's Sampler of graduate degrees only serves to make the student look ill informed. If the multidegree trajectory is born of indecision rather than overambition, the student is better served by just being honest about the indecision.

- Undercredentialing: *"Once I get my MD from Hollywood Upstairs Medical School, I plan to begin my career with Médecins Sans Frontières."* This phenomenon occurs less often, but it is still common enough to be a concern. Students need to demonstrate that they understand the reality of their situation. If a top-tier graduate program is not within their reach, their career goals should match their future credentials. If the student plans a career within international organizations, the student should select a top-tier program that will have international cachet.

- Puffery: *"Third-Tier University is simply the best place to get an MPA."* We see this most often when students want to attend a school for reasons other than academic reputation. Perhaps they want to stay local to continue political involvement, to be near family, or for financial reasons. Readers would much rather an explicit statement of intent than an attempt to convince them that every ranking available of MPA programs is wrong.

- Web-page speak: *"MBA degrees present the single best outside-the-box way to have impactful, dynamic change in the synergistic paradigm of the public sector."* Students must be critical consumers of graduate school information. Parroting back slogans from graduate school web pages or school brochures is a sure way to have a reader scrawl "naive" all over the comment sheet. For obvious reasons, students who propose MBA programs tend to fall for this trick most often. Truman's preference against MBA programs has been stated before, but should advisors have the rare student for whom the MBA makes sense, they should encourage that student not to play Business Buzzword Bingo with the application.[11]

- Omission: *"I plan to go directly to law school. I have no latent desire to study in the United Kingdom even if someone else is paying."* Students who plan to apply to a UK scholarship program or take time to work before graduate school or get a Fulbright to Argentina should put that in Question 11. There is no reason why any of these plans would make the foundation less likely to award the Truman; in most cases we would be more likely to award it. If students have other constraints on their graduate school plans—military service, financial considerations, family obligations—these should be included in Question 11.

- Imprecise language: *"A JD is the best degree to prepare me for my career in education policy."* This issue arises most often with those students who want to get professional degrees but do not want to ever act as members of that profession. The bulk of the student's application focuses on policy concerns, but Question 11 still contains a trip to law or medical school. It is often difficult to determine whether this problem is one of degree selection—perhaps the student does not quite understand the value of a policy degree—or one of sloppy writing. Students who submit applications with this issue should prepare for the eventuality of being interrogated on the difference between a policy degree and a professional degree.

- Wasted space: *"While in law school, I plan to take the first year, or 1L, curriculum which includes . . ."* The reading committee is comprised of a variety of people from a variety of backgrounds. Several of them are graduate school admissions officers or deans. A few even attended the program that the student is writing about. There is no reason to approach an essay about Harvard Law School as if we are wholly unfamiliar with Harvard or the study of law. This issue is the most frustrating. We often never hear the student's motivations because we are too busy reading through a listing of core course work.

- Dense space: *"A Masters in Embedded Systems from the KTH Royal Institute of Technology would, of course, be the best choice for me."* The inverse of wasted space finds readers with degree programs that are wholly unfamiliar. These programs are often highly technical and specialized, which often means that students come from insulated programs and do not always know that regular people have no idea what computational neurobiology is. Help students to identify which programs are lesser known and suggest ways to explain these programs for a lay audience.

- Failure to show work: *"I will attend medical school in Sweden."* For most students, writing a response to Question 11 requires a lot of thinking and research. Yet so many students do not feel compelled to share that information. If the program the student identified begs a question like "why not an MPH?" or "do you even speak Swedish?", the student can save readers some confusion and save the interview panelists some time by including that information.

- Failure to persuade: *"My choice of law school has the highest judicial clerkship placement in the country."* This is the inverse to "failure to show work." In an effort to demonstrate all the research they have done, as well as a reflection of the odd things that one can find on the Internet, students are beginning to incorporate some truly unpersuasive factoids into these essays. During one review cycle, I saw this example sentence in three separate essays—none of them were for the same school. Such bits of ridiculata serve only to pad the essay and provide little context.

- Failure to address deficiencies: *"Pay no attention to the lack of quantitative course work behind the curtain."* Readers are well aware of the general qualifications required to get into these graduate school programs. An applicant missing some crucial component should address this item briefly in Question 11. A simple acknowledgment that the student needs to take additional course work or will have to overcome a lack of professional experience will only serve to enhance the essay and demonstrate that the student has done appropriate research.

- Failure to address uncertainty: *"Even though I haven't taken a single course in economics, the PhD in Applied Economics is for me!"* Believe it or not, it is perfectly acceptable for a student to express some uncertainty in the application. A student who is willing to grapple with these issues, rather than blindly charging into the fray, can be a compelling candidate.

Once the student's application is in perfect shape, then advisors need only to determine the best way to memorialize all of that hard work. In general, readers do not need a lot of information about the degree program in the letter of nomination. But the nomination letter might be the better place to address deficiencies in detail. If advisors know that a student lacks strong economics course work but plans to take it next semester, they can introduce that idea early to reassure the readers that these issues are being resolved. The nomination letter is also a good place to discuss the research the student did to select the degree—particularly if the student lacks room to do so coherently. Finally, be certain that the degree that is described in the Institution Nomination Letter is the same as the one proposed by the student. If a student proposes an MPP, the letter should mirror that language.

Conclusion: Our Little Secret

After all this work—the gnashing of teeth and rending of garments, the soul-searching talks and extensive research, the informational interviews and coaching—it turns out that the foundation does not really care if the student ever gets the degree proposed.

In fact, we spend much of our early relationship with students trying to get them to think about other degree paths and programs. We cajole them into taking years off. We hector them about switching degrees, dropping the joint program, or adding another degree. We undo all of the advisor's precious work.

But in the end, the scholars and our program are better for it. Graduate school advising is a moving target. But by encouraging critical thinking about graduate school from the beginning of the application process, advisors are ensuring the next generation of public service leaders is prepared for the challenges ahead, even if one of the first challenges is trying to get the Truman review committee to agree to their joint degree programs.

8

When the Abyss Stares Back
The Eldritch Horror of the "Additional Information" Prompt

TARA YGLESIAS

Sometimes the most frightening things are those that defy description. The undefined or the unseen can be used to terrify and unsettle. Shirley Jackson, best among others, frightened readers with random wall knocks and the never-innocent question "whose hand was I holding?"[1] H. P. Lovecraft built an entire career on vague piles of tentacles.[2] That "looming spectre of inutterable horror"[3] creates fear by injecting disorder and confusion into our orderly existence.

Perhaps no one is more susceptible to the creeping sense of dread brought about by the unknown than high-achieving college students. They have done the planning, the research, the mock interviews. They have answered the questions that ask what they might be doing in August of 2055. They have developed three separate graduate school trajectories—and contacted the relevant thesis supervisors. They are not interested in mystery. But then, at application's end, they realize with a dawning sense of terror that the application has gone meta to ask if there is anything, anything at all really, that we might also like to know?

The Truman application is by no means alone in this particular jump scare. Even college admission applications have a little "so . . . anything else?" at the end. But if the complaints by Truman Scholars are any indication, this question is the most anxiety-inducing on our application. They worry they did not answer the question correctly even though there is no correct answer. And if the complaints from readers are any indication, this question produces a fair bit of anxiety for them as well. Their concerns range from not knowing what they should do with the information the applicant provides to fondly reminiscing on the time when the question was optional. Even a cursory review of those applicants not selected for interview suggests this prompt is often misunderstood and usually underutilized.[4]

If neither the applicants nor the readers are happy with the responses to Question 14, this suggests our guidance on this question comes across less as generous latitude and more as sinister, unrelenting fog. This essay will discuss why we ask such an open-ended question, as well as confront some of the urban legends surrounding our motives. The article provides guidance on helpful and less helpful types of responses, with a special focus on the particular issues surrounding students who may have difficult or traumatic responses to the additional information prompt. Finally, it covers how best to advise applicants on selecting a topic for this prompt as well as general tips on effective presentation.

It Begins: On the Origins of Question 14

Every good monster comes with an origin story, and Question 14 is no exception. The Truman application has always included a bit of space at the end for additional information. By 1990, this question had become "15. What additional personal information do you wish to share with the Truman Scholarship Foundation? (optional)." After the application moved online in the early 2000s, the foundation removed the words "personal"[5] and "optional"[6] and renumbered the application so this prompt became Question 14.

Question 14—the now relatively straightforward "What additional information do you wish to share with the Truman Foundation?"[7]—may have changed slightly in wording, but the intent behind the question was always the same. We viewed the question as a leveler of sorts and most often discussed its importance to non-traditional applicants. The purpose of the question was to give the transfer student, the returning student, the student with academic woes, a place to explain. Question 14 would give those applicants the opportunity to bolster their application, to deal with an issue that was likely going to prevent them from advancing.[8] We thought this option was especially important for those students at institutions where the nomination letter was unlikely to be strong.[9]

For applicants without extenuating circumstances, Question 14 was meant to provide a space for them to tell reviewers an interesting fact that might lead to a discussion in an interview. We assumed that any exceptional applicant would leap at the chance to share one additional, likely exceptional, fact about themselves.

The problem with this intent was that it was not communicated very well. Applicants (and advisors) did not know what the foundation was looking for. Some left the question blank. Others attempted to use it as a tiny personal statement or abridged personal manifesto. Some either ascribed to it the motives of other applications or guessed what reviewers might want. As a result, Question 14 was referred to by some as the "hardship question" or the "diversity question."

There is some truth to the hardship sobriquet. One of the stated purposes of the question was to give space to an applicant whose experiences could not be accurately captured in the standard application.[10] Question 14 was meant to provide some measure of equity. For example, the applicant who could not be as involved in campus activities because of family obligations could use Question 14 to explain that situation—something not covered elsewhere in the application.

Those students who did not have a hardship to discuss were not disadvantaged. But applicants believed that they were. One scholar wrote an essay about his parent's divorce—which he said was not all that traumatic —in an effort to provide the expected hardship. He felt he needed the story to explain the lone "B" on his transcript (no one had questions about it). Applicants seemed actively disappointed not to have hardship to discuss or deficiencies to explain. Others shied away from the application entirely, feeling that without such a story they would be unlikely to prevail.

Similarly, many applicants believed that Question 14 was a diversity question. On some applications, there is a space, usually at the end, to provide information related to diversity factors. Some applications are explicit about requesting this information while others provide diversity factors as a suggestion for content.

Due to a series of tedious and byzantine government regulations,

Truman is not permitted to ask questions relating to diversity criteria as these are not standards for selection.[11] Thus, Question 14 was never intended to be a question about diversity. While selecting a diverse class across a number of factors, including both statutorily recognized characteristics as well as other items that are vital to our program,[12] is an important goal of the foundation, we are constrained around whether or how we can directly gather such information.[13]

This is not to say that an essay about either hardship or diversity would be misplaced as a response to Question 14. Applicants have written very effectively about the challenges they have faced or discussed how their identity relates to their interests and service. But the intent behind the question was far narrower. Outside of a few very specific instances, we are looking for an essay that is more icebreaker than heartbreaker.

Be Afraid. Be Very Afraid.

Given that Question 14 at least started out as optional (and still reads like so many other optional prompts), applicants and advisors would be forgiven for thinking the question was not important. While the plot twist here is not that Question 14 is critical to a successful application,[14] but that it is a very significant essay for a certain type of student.[15] At the very least, Question 14 is the opportunity for any applicant to personalize the application and show an authentic self. There is really no argument for leaving the question blank.

Having required everyone to jump into the abyss of Question 14, the Truman Foundation is much more explicit about what we want—even though what we want has not changed. Applicants should first use Question 14 to answer questions they anticipate the foundation might have or deal with issues in their application. But, for the vast majority of applicants, Question 14 is their opportunity to explore anything else that they did not cover in detail elsewhere in the application. Then the question becomes the vast, yawning horror described in the opening. Applicants could, in theory, write about anything! Unfortunately, our stock guidance is exactly that: they should write about anything.

Of course, anything is not really *any thing*. We expect an exceptional student to produce an exceptional response, and the question does garner essays that cover other award-worthy interests: world-record-breaking jump-roping, nationally recognized piano playing, critically lauded photography. We receive brief, incisive essays on the applicant's home town, charming missives about obscure hobbies, or thoughtful narratives about the development of an applicant's interest. Question 14 is also the perfect place for a student to discuss an impressive leadership or public service activity that was too remote in time or otherwise did not fit into the application elsewhere.

The common thread to these essays is that whatever is revealed is just the sort of thing one might add as a prelude to a conversation: "This is Sasha. They do jigsaw puzzles competitively. I didn't even know that was a thing." It is no mystery why many of the topics covered in Question 14 provide fodder for interview questions.

The party introduction is also a good litmus test for responses we do not wish to see in Question 14:

- *They really need this scholarship.* General pleas for the scholarship are usually not compelling. Everyone who applies has need—either financial or professional (or both).[15] A generic essay that explains how important the award is to the applicant is not helpful to the reader. These essays often resort to vague predictions—"if I don't get the Truman, I cannot go to law school"—which at best overstate the value of the award and at worst attempt to suggest Truman is responsible for a dystopian future. This essay is distinct from one where an applicant explains an issue that resulted from financial hardship ("my ability to join extracurriculars suffered because of my need to work to support my family"), but even then, applicants should confine themselves to the specific facts of the situation they are explaining and not feel compelled to belabor the details of their financial situation.
- *They are really good people.* Similarly, essays that speak in general terms about an applicant's interest in public service are not helpful. The foundation receives many, many dozens of these—often centered around the hoary premise of "to whom much is given, much is required." These essays often lack action and fact in favor of rhetorical flourish. Even an essay of heartbreakingly good quality would be useless unless it were specific to the applicant.
- *They know really good people.* Essays detailing the public service

exploits of the applicant's relatives or peers provide little insight into the applicant before us. There is certainly a place to discuss personal history or family as it relates to a public service career, but readers are most interested in the actions of the person actually applying for the award.

- *They can quote, at length, from other really good people.* The foundation receives a fair number of essays that attempt to explain a student's interest via a lengthy quote, usually poetry. These essays often leave the reader impressed with the words of someone else rather than the applicant.
- *Here are some select quotes from their Tinder profile.* Applicants sometimes mistake charming personal qualities for essay-worthy content. Items that pop up on a social media profile ("avid flosser!" "5th degree vegan!") are probably best left there. As goes the advice for every other Truman essay, if five thousand people could write the exact same essay on the horrors of being a tall woman, select another topic.
- *They would like to apologize for all the things they have.* These sorts of essays are an off-shoot of people assuming Question 14 is supposed to be about hardship. Applicants instead provide bizarre recitations of everything good in their life, followed by the suggestion that these items are somehow burdens, hampering their ability to win the Truman. Recognizing and thinking critically about one's privilege can be an insightful experience, but one hard to reduce to two thousand characters. Complaining about the burdens of privilege while actively courting a university's nomination for a competitive fellowship also seems ill-conceived.
- *They would like to draw attention to this minor failing.* It is entirely understandable that applicants would want the application to be perfect. But too many applicants spend Question 14 detailing some perceived weakness rather than speaking of their strengths in a compelling way. Apologizing for a lone B-, begging for forgiveness over not being overly enamored with partisan politics, donning a hairshirt over a thin record of internships are not good uses of Question 14. Some of these reek of humblebrag ("Sorry for my dense transcript, I couldn't decide on just one major!") while others should be handed off to a qualified therapist ("No one but me is

responsible for my poor showing of a B- in Beginning Latin Dance. I have asked myself many times why I failed to commit all I could to this elective. In this TED Talk, I will . . .”). Regardless, these responses often draw attention to an item best left undiscussed.[16]

- *This is Harry. His parents were murdered by Voldemort.* Applicants sometimes disclose items in Question 14 that detail traumatic experiences. These essays can seem uncomfortable for the applicant and often reflect a palpable reluctance to reveal the experience. Such essays are almost certainly uncomfortable for the reader and usually result in their agonizing over what precisely to do with such revealing personal information. Often unmoored from the rest of the application, these answers can be awkward and unhelpful. Outside of certain, limited circumstances—where the disclosure is both necessary for the reader to understand the application fully and the applicant is comfortable disclosing the experience—these items should not be covered in the Truman application.

Nonetheless, we see many essays—most ineffective—that reveal all manner of trauma being visited on the applicant. Interestingly, applicants often express a reluctance to write about these experiences, and readers express displeasure at having to read them. Applicants (and advisors) need to exercise much better judgement around when and how to disclose trauma in these types of applications.

Part of the problem stems from a misunderstanding of the criteria used to evaluate both Question 14 and the application as a whole. While there are some Truman Scholars who prevail based on a record of uniform excellence, there are many who win the award, in part, due to distance traveled. Within this latter group, we often find inspirational stories of hardship and tragedy overcome.

These scholars can present compelling narratives that are likely to be highlighted in the press or social media, but it would be a mistake to reduce these winners to just their traumatic stories. In many cases, the stories were not even known to the foundation at the time of selection. Other times, the stories are an afterthought—we are much more focused on the scholar's record of achievement and plans for the future.

Truman staff bear some responsibility for this confusion, in part because we have highlighted the moving stories of some of the scholars.

We should take better care to explain that what is prominent on social media is not necessarily reflective of what is discussed during the selection process. To do otherwise does a disservice to these students and suggests their achievements are secondary.

For scholars, revealing these experiences can also create a scenario in which they are unsure whether they won the award on merit or because of an awful thing that happened to them. Take as an example a scholar we worked with on an application for another award. She was struggling with disclosing a traumatic event that was intimately connected to the work she wanted to do. She had not disclosed this information in her Truman application, although she was told to do so by her advisor. The advisor felt that if she disclosed this trauma, she would certainly win.

Take a moment to gasp.

We know this advisor. This advice was not cynical—this advice was the very reasonable interpretation of what seems to win awards. From the perspective of the advisor, knowing what happened to this woman makes a lot of things fall into place. The experience she had explains a great deal about who she is and how she navigates the work she does. And yet, even without knowing, the reader can see she is amazing and accomplished in her own right.

The scholar told the foundation that she feels dishonest when she shares this experience—almost as if she is trying to gain sympathy. As a result, she does not always feel deserving of the accolades she receives when she shares it. She feels that people take her more seriously because of the traumatic event, and she is not convinced that gravitas is warranted. While a traumatic experience can sometimes lead to understanding and empathy, it may not be a substitute for expertise. But if she chooses not to disclose the information, she feels that she is being coy about her reasons for doing the work she does. Hers is a thorny dilemma for any advisor— and she is by no means unique in this quandary.

There are probably as many good reasons as not to disclose this kind of information, but only the student bears the weight of that decision. Anyone taking the time to read this far into an essay on one question of the Truman scholarship application is well familiar with a student-cen- tered process, but it is worthwhile to make certain that advisors are focused on the student when dealing with issues this sensitive. Allowing the student to process all the available information and make their own decision regarding disclosure might not guarantee application quality, but it will leave the student with a most positive impression of the process.

This misunderstanding and our over-reliance on these trauma-narrative essays can also have some real consequences for those applicants without traumatic experiences. We hear often from students who feel unworthy of accolades or, more troublingly, unworthy of recognition as a student with a particular identity, because they lack a traumatic experience. For example, we selected a young woman whose father was Black and her mother white. She was raised in a rural community where her family was one of very few nonwhite families. She described her upbringing as happy and her community, while not perfect, as mostly accepting. She often spoke of how she struggled to frame this experience both in her Truman application and in her field: How could she work on issues of inclusion when she lacked first-hand knowledge of the bias and bigotry others suffer?

This form of gatekeeping, in which one must have personally experienced suffering in order to be perceived as qualified to understand or help address it, is counterproductive to student development, let alone the application process. Students who are afraid that their journeys or identities are not enough are misunderstanding what these awards are designed to celebrate. There is no threshold of suffering before a student can be considered. Rather than minimizing their own experience, or worse, trying to unearth nonexistent trauma, applicants would be better served trying to articulate what drew them to an issue in the first place.

On Vanquishing the Nameless Abyss

As a former Truman Scholar, I have first-hand experience with Question 14. My grades were terrible. Not terrible by any objective standard; I was coming in hot around a 3.4 or so, but by 1990s Truman standards, my grades were abysmal. I had gentleman's C's, and I was obviously not a gentleman. So when the time came to actually cut and paste my additional information, I was told that I needed to write about why my grades were so bad.[17] Problem was, I did not think they were so bad. I was a first-generation college student who went to a not-great high school where "doesn't get into fights" was synonymous with "college material." I had no idea how to study or how to navigate college until a friend told me during the second semester of my freshman year.[18] I earned (mostly) A's thereafter.

But this was not an interesting story to me. It seemed routine and boring. I wanted to talk about the things that interested me—why I wanted to work with kids in the criminal justice system, since it was not obvious in my application. I wanted to tell stories about being a DJ or throwing ceramics or starting a coven.[19] But I agreed with my advisors and wrote a lengthy apology for my grades sprinkled with just enough personal detail to make me sound interesting but not wholly pathetic.

During an interview for another scholarship while I was performing "About That B- in International Relations, Reprise," a panelist interrupted me. He said I was much more interesting than mistakes I made four years ago. I blinked a few times . . . and told them the story about the coven. The story went over terrifically—it killed and I got the award.

Years later, I looked at my Truman score sheets. One reader had scrawled "her grades are fine, what's the big deal?" and another wrote "why is she interested in juvenile justice?" And then, I saw those dreaded words "This response is unhelpful." The fact that I was selected for interview was nearly a miss—in part because the foundation evaluated GPA differently at that time (and no amount of explaining was going to fix that), and in part because there were gaps in my application that I failed to address.

I tell this story for a few reasons. First, I am fairly typical of many Truman applicants. Of the foundation's three elements—leadership, service and academics—these applicants are usually only strong in two. Most often, these are excellent service and academics with weaker leadership, but sometimes they look like my strain of decent service and leadership with messy grades.[20] The conversation I had with my advisor and seemingly every single Truman Scholar who ever set foot on my university campus is likely one most advisors will have again and again: How does an applicant determine what the readers want to hear in Question 14? At what point are advisors doing their job helpfully and appropriately versus drawing attention to an issue no one cares about until the applicant makes them care?

Second, my story highlights the limits of conventional wisdom. My advisor and I assumed that we needed to add drama—in the form of spotlighting my shortcomings and discussing my struggles—in order to be interesting. If we came up with this strategy before the era of reality TV, I shudder to think how much this concept has expanded.[21] Little did we realize that the drama of a scholarship application is inherent in the questions. The excitement comes from the applicant's potential and the fact that what happens next is a mystery to both the foundation and the applicant, regardless of how detailed their plan in Questions 11 through 13.[22]

Question 14 is the place where the messy application can be redeemed. It can make up for ineffective letters of recommendation or unclear motivations or confusing trajectories. Again, that is not to say Question 14 can make or break the application, but it can tip the scales in favor of a candidate if used effectively. Question 14 is far more than an optional throwaway.

Selecting a topic for Question 14 may be the most iterative part of the application process. Advisors should begin by ensuring none of the usual suspects need to be addressed by the applicant:

- *Transfer or non-traditional students.* Students who transferred after significant time at another institution and non-traditional students may need to discuss this situation in Question 14.[23] Non-traditional students in particular seem to make effective use of Question 14 when they are able to highlight their prior leadership or service that may be too remote in time for inclusion in the prior leadership (Question 7) and service questions (Question 8).
- *Confusing career path or academic trajectory.* If applicants go from one path to another or seem to be headed in every direction at once, they will likely need to gather these threads together in Question 14. In some cases, these situations can be covered in the nomination letter, but it is often more compelling to hear from the applicant themselves.
- *Disruption in program of study or activity level.* In general, any obvious change in grades, activity or program of study should be addressed somewhere in the application. Straightforward items (change of major or temporary illness) can be explained in the nomination letter or a supporting recommendation letter. Anything more in-depth would likely need to be explained by the applicant. One exception: If the disruption in question is something the student does not wish to talk about, the Truman representative may

cover it in the nomination letter and note that fact. The applicant should approve this approach.

If applicants do not have an item within one of these categories, they are now free to write about anything at all. Some suggestions to consider:

- *Now What?* Unless it is self-explanatory (and likely to remain so even after someone has read many dozens of these applications in a short period of time), applicants need to explain what the foundation should do with the information they are providing in Question 14. If readers are to glean from their Question 14 something about their character or their likelihood of prevailing through a difficult graduate school program, they need to say so explicitly. Again, given the time frame allotted to review applications and the number to sift through, readers will not have the ability to extrapolate the reasoning behind the response to Question 14. Applicants should be explicit. This advice is especially true if the applicant is disclosing something traumatic that appears to have nothing to do with the application.

- *The Kindness of Strangers.* Chances are good that a third party will need to be enlisted for this process. Very few advisors—and even fewer applicants—are capable of reviewing these applications and immediately sensing what readers might need to be told in Question 14. Applicants should give their materials to someone who does not know them well. If this person cannot summarize the applicant's history and goals accurately, the gap in that understanding is the topic for Question 14.

- *About That "B."* Other readers should also be helpful in determining *whether* an issue in the application needs to be addressed. Stated application criteria should also provide guidance. Applicants often want to explain good, solid grades as if they were embarrassing—despite the fact that the foundation is clear in saying that grades are not terribly important. There is little harm in overexplaining, but it is a shame when an applicant explains the obvious and does not discuss other, more interesting things.

- *There Will Be Follow-Ups.* If an applicant writes about something in Question 14, interviewers assume we are permitted to ask questions about it. While we are not in the business of probing obviously sensitive issues during the interview, we may ask a question to clarify. In other cases, we may not be aware that an issue is sensitive. Applicants sometimes write essays that seem detached but actually trigger very strong feelings in the stress of an interview room.[25] Be certain that if students write about an experience or issue, they are able to talk about it without breaking down. If they cannot do so, but the foundation still needs to be aware of an issue, a note in the advisor's nomination letter would be sufficient: "Applicant's mother is currently very ill and, as a result, their grades have suffered. They find this difficult to talk about but wanted the committee to be aware." As always, make sure the student is comfortable with providing this information.

- *Context Matters.* Just like every other response, context is important. The vague nature of Question 14 seems to encourage similarly vague responses. Readers still need to understand the context in which these events occur. Some of the very best Question 14 responses provide context for where the applicant is from. These sorts of essays can often help to create cohesion as well as provide answers for perennial questions of what drew this applicant to this issue. Providing context also helps to ground the generic "I'm a Good Person" essays into something easier to evaluate.

- *Just One Thing.* Likewise, it is a mistake to try to put too much into Question 14. The response is limited to 2,000 characters, plus spaces. The old debate adage—only go for one issue in rebuttal—applies here. Applicants sometimes decide to cover every potential question or detail every important activity and that rarely works. There simply is not enough space to cover more than one issue effectively. Minor issues could be covered in a nomination letter or a letter of recommendation, freeing up space for the applicant to be more substantive.

- *Administrative Details.* Items like a lack of relevant coursework available at the student's institution, one incomplete or aberrant grade or an obvious course of study that was rejected for practical reasons could be dealt with in the nomination letter. Generally, if the issues are administrative, it is fine for advisors to cover those briefly. But if the issue is one that is more substantive—

relevant coursework exists but the student chose not to take it, for instance—reviewers likely need students to explain this decision in their own words.

- *Privacy*. Applicants should be aware that, while the foundation exercises caution with the application, no system is perfect. Foundation policy is that the only people able to see the application are those who need to do so in performance of their duties, but that will still include several people. If a student has an especially sensitive issue, the Truman representative may want to reach out to our office for guidance on whether or how to discuss it. Particularly for issues relating to the honor code or ethical or criminal matters, the foundation may have recommendations for disclosure to prevent widespread dissemination.

- *Uniqueness*. Much like with every other essay, applicants should avoid writing an essay that could be written by any other candidate. In 2020, COVID-19 disrupted every campus and every student. It is a shared generational experience and unlikely to yield useful information for an essay. The injustice of a cancelled internship or capricious university grading policy can be covered briefly by a nomination letter. Heartwarming essays on the virtues of social distancing will add little to our understanding of an applicant. Even applicants who experience the more tragic consequences of COVID-19 should not feel compelled to address these in their Question 14 if other topics are better discussed.

Just When You Think It's Safe to Go Back in the Application

Much like any quality horror film, Question 14 seems to spring back to life again even after the written application is complete and submitted. At the end of every Truman interview, Question 14 is made flesh again, this time in the form of the final minute—usually prefaced with "is there anything else you'd like to tell us?"

Fortunately for all concerned, interviewers fully expect the answer to be "No. Thank You." Unlike Question 14 on the application, which provides the opportunity to equalize or expand on the universe of knowledge about the applicant, the end of interview question has no such pretensions.

Interviewers are happy to have either a quick update ("I was selected for a summer internship with the State Department!"), a return to an earlier question ("I finally remembered the name of my favorite book!"—it happens) or a simple "This has been fun/not fun/exquisitely painful. Thank you!"

The purpose of this question is to allow the finalist to leave the interview on their terms. If they felt as if the interview went well, they can leave on the high note of kindly thanking the interviewers and confidently pushing their chair back. If they have felt unable to string together coherent sentences for most of the interview, they can now recite something prepared and leave the interview feeling better about the experience. So this open-ended question still contains a whiff of the abyss, hopefully without inducing full panic.

Well, Clarice, Have the Applicants Stopped Screaming?

Question 14 should be nothing to fear. A true Frankenstein's monster, it was designed to be helpful only to turn terror-inducing when misunderstood. The question was never intended to be a trick, or to apply only to certain applicants in certain situations. Question 14 was meant to provide applicants the opportunity to introduce themselves—their successes, their dreams and sometimes their failures—to a panel of people who are genuinely excited to meet them.

The foundation hopes that applicants now use this opportunity as it was intended. For many, it will be the opportunity to provide readers with yet another impressive feat or interesting anecdote. For others, it will be a chance to show how far they have come or how far they plan to go. For a few, answering this question may require discussing unpleasant facts, but the point is not to dwell there.

As with any part of the application, there are dozens of little details that separate a successful Question 14 from an unsuccessful one. But unlike the average horror movie, one false move will not doom the candidate.[26]

9

Enough about Me, What Do You Think about Me?
Surviving the Truman Interview

TARA YGLESIAS

Few things can derail an accomplished candidate or an otherwise reasonable faculty advisor quite like an interview experience that turns out to be unsuccessful. This disappointment is acute and often lasting. For candidates, the experience can sour everything they learned during the process. For advisors, an unsuccessful interview, particularly for a favored candidate, can lead to a full-blown existential crisis. The Truman Foundation often deals with the fallout from these experiences—most often in the form of faculty advisors who call to find out what they might have done differently.

In most cases the answer is the always-unfulfilling nothing. The difference between a Truman Finalist and a Truman Scholar is often one of tiny margins wholly outside the control of the advisor and, in some cases, the candidate. Understanding the uncontrollable nature of the interview process is vital to understanding both how best to prepare candidates for the experience and how to deal with the outcome.

This essay discusses the nature of the interviews, provides suggestions for candidate preparation, and offers advice for dealing with the aftermath. Though much of this material is generic to many interview situations, the lessons learned are mainly drawn from the Truman interview process.

The Interview: Fickle Food on a Shifting Plate

If a school is able to produce finalists with some regularity, the institution's Truman program is both identifying the right candidates and presenting the students in the best possible light. The Truman Foundation considers having finalists, not scholars, to be a true marker of the success of an individual institution. We realize universities may feel differently.

We make this distinction because once advisors have (repeatedly) hit the submit button on a student's application, their part in the process—the part that is controlled, monitored, and knowable—is over. Advisors can work with students to craft prose of heartbreakingly excellent quality. Recommendation letters can provide compelling and vibrant details. The Truman faculty representative can write the single best letter of nomination ever, moving the committee to rapturous tears. Advisors can even channel Lydia Grant during mock interviews ("You want the Truman? Well, the Truman costs. And right here is where you start paying—in sweat."), but advisors are controlling only the preparation of the candidate. Preparation will go only so far and does not guarantee results.

Even the best-prepared finalist is at the whim of the inherently subjective interview process. Yes, I used the *s*-word. Although we provide our panelists with explicit instructions about our criteria, do our best to guard against interviewer bias, and endeavors to give each finalist the same consideration, the process necessarily has subjective elements.[1]

Understanding the nature of the Truman interview begins with a thorough—and likely somewhat dull—explanation of the interview process. Panelists receive the applications about two weeks prior to the interview date. Along with the applications, we send guidance, a list of suggested questions, and a copy of the Bulletin of Information.[2] We provide a schedule and a blank form to allow the panelists to write comments or, if they wish, score the materials.

The guidance given to the panelists begins by reminding them that they are the foundation's "investment committee." The choice of words is deliberate. By naming a student as a Truman Scholar, the panelists will require the investment of a good deal of foundation resources. It may come as a surprise to those outside the process, but panelists are not evil dream-crushers. If we permitted it, our panelists would give every finalist a scholarship of some sort. We must remind them of their role and the sobering reality that they have only a few scholarships to award. We provide panelists with guidance in their decision making, including the following list of attributes that all Truman Scholars must possess.

- *Likelihood of becoming a change agent.* Finalists work well with others to affect public policy or to exert leadership so that others follow their lead.
- *Commitment to a career in public service.* Finalists have the values, ambitions, and desires that seem likely to lead to a career in public service. The foundation defines public service as employment in government at any level, uniformed services, public interest organizations, nongovernmental research and/or educational organizations, public and private schools, and public service–oriented nonprofit organizations, such as those whose primary purposes are to help needy or disadvantaged persons or to protect the environment.
- *Ability to hold their own at the proposed graduate or professional school.* A recommender could write an enthusiastic recommendation to the dean of this school. The person need not become an academic star at the institution.
- *Heart and compassion.* The primary concern of the candidate is with the welfare of others and not with personal ego nor self-aggrandizement.

These criteria are the same as those listed on the website and drilled into the collective consciousness during any of countless NAFA appearances. The order of the criteria is significant as well; the leadership and service components are paramount.

In terms of interview guidance, panelists are asked to spend no more than five to seven minutes becoming familiar with a candidate's application and policy proposal. Instead, panelists are encouraged to ask provocative questions in the candidate's general field. Panelists are repeatedly instructed to give the students a challenging interview. They take these instructions very seriously.

The foundation does not send along any information from its readers, the Finalist Selection Committee. The applications are transmitted to panelists without comments or scores. Panelists are explicitly instructed to come to their own conclusions about the written materials. We also do not require panelists to score the materials, although nearly all panelists arrive with the applications ranked or scored in some fashion.

Prior to the 2012 cycle, panelists were notified if the Finalist Selection Committee judged an application to be outstanding. The outstanding rating was rarely given—of the six hundred applications a year, fewer than ten received this designation. Based on panelist feedback, the foundation eliminated this practice. Panelists felt that this designation put too much pressure on the performance of the applicant.

By the day of the interview, most panelists will have spent quite a bit of time poring over the applications. They generally arrive with lists of questions and extensive notes. All are genuinely enthusiastic to meet the finalists and hand out as many Truman Scholarships as possible. The foundation's greatest challenge is to keep the panelists from handing out too many scholarships.

The day begins with an orientation, both for the panelists and the finalists. The panelist orientation is usually quite short, with a member of the foundation's staff going over the marching orders for the day. Many panelists are veterans of the process, either as panelists or as Truman Scholars. Much of the panel's orientation time is spent catching up with old friends rather than actively planning how to make a finalist's life miserable.

The orientation with the finalists takes a bit longer.[3] The panelists introduce themselves and go over the schedule for the day. As someone focused on process, I review the entire day in what can be described only as a comic level of detail. Sharing specific and extensive information about the interview process with all finalists is another attempt to level the playing field. The foundation does not want a student who comes from a school without a robust Truman program to spend the morning fretting over whether there will be water while a student from a school with an established Truman program comfortably reads affirming text messages from a kindly faculty advisor. We accept that there will always be inequalities, but access to information about our process should not be one of them.

After whipping the finalists into a frenzy of anticipation, the panelists adjourn to begin the interviews. Prior to a candidate's interview, we may discuss the application generally. We usually settle on a first question or, at least, a person who is tasked with the first question. From there the interview is entirely unscripted. We do not settle on an order of questions.

We do not discuss who is going to ask questions about which topics. We just see where the interview takes us.

This may cause some finalists and their advisors to recoil in horror—because this part is where things get fuzzy. The flow of the interview depends on both the mood of the panel and the response of the person being interviewed. This statement seems obvious, but understanding and accepting this point is critical to understanding the interview process and preparing students to effectively present themselves.

We have only twenty minutes with each finalist, so when the student gets into the room, we go right to work. Although some panels and certain panelists will lob a "how are you?" at a finalist, usually we immediately start with substantive questions. The types of questions greatly vary with different panels and individual panelists, but there are a few constants:

- *We spend very little time rehashing materials in the application (e.g., can you describe exactly how you cured malaria?).* If we do ask these types of questions, they are likely needed to clarify something in the application and will be dealt with quickly.
- *There are no trick questions.* We want to hear the finalists' answer, not what they think we want to hear. Panelists will often play devil's advocate (and occasionally *devil's* devil's advocate). There is no way to guess how a panelist might personally feel about an issue, and the next panelist might feel another way entirely. Truman interviews are about understanding the passion of the finalist, not about exploring the views of the panelists. Finalists should just answer the question.
- *There are no wrong answers, even if the answer is actually wrong.* Many successful Truman Finalists have answered questions inarticulately, incompletely, or incorrectly. The Truman interview is not a dissertation defense. We do not expect a finalist to know everything about an issue. Answering "I don't know" is appropriate (indeed, preferred) when finalists find themselves on thin ice.
- *We do not (usually) mind when finalists change the subject.* Panels will sometimes get on to a topic and not let it go. It is appropriate to respond to a question and then use the response as a way to redirect the conversation. If panelists are not finished with a topic, they are quick to let students know.
- *Questions cannot be interpreted as anything other than questions.*

Some finalists spend a lot of time rehashing the interview and trying to draw conclusions from the questions asked ("They asked only one question about my policy proposal. They hate me!"). The type and the variety of questions mean nothing.

At the eighteen-minute mark (a bit earlier if a finalist tends to have long answers, a bit later if the answers were shorter), a panelist will announce that it is the last question. After finalists respond to the last question, they will be permitted to close the interview on their own terms. Although the finalists know this portion of the interview is coming, it still seems to throw several of them into a panic. There are a few things to keep in mind about the closing statement:

- *A good, bad, or indifferent closing is not going to change the outcome.* Finalists have delivered dreadful, lengthy, quote-filled soliloquies and still won. Others have moved me to the point where I came close to tears. Most finalists, win or lose, offer just fine closing statements. The only thing the closing statement can do is make the student feel good (or not) about the experience.
- *It should not be a "statement."* Brief and in keeping with the tone of the interview is the best policy. Students may be relieved that they made it through *The Rime of the Ancient Mariner* by memory, but panelists probably did not radiate good vibes on their way out.
- *It can simply be, "Thanks! This was fun!"* Some of the most successful statements are those in which finalists thank the panel, honestly say whether it was as bad as they expected, and reflect on that moment.
- *Questions or suggestions are best saved for later.* Some students have turned around and asked the panel a question. This tactic never goes well, as the thunderous confused silence seems to chase the finalist right out the room. Others have used the time to suggest ways for the process to be improved. Since many of the panelists have only limited exposure to the inner workings of the application process, well-meaning suggestions are often met with brow furrowing and panicked glances. Again, asking questions is not the best way to close an interview.[4]
- *Finalists should not cry.* This is not because it has an impact on a

finalist's application in any way but because it makes everyone deeply uncomfortable.

After candidates leave, the panelists briefly talk about them while they are still fresh in our memory, usually mentioning a few strengths or things to consider. After this quick chat, we move to the next finalist. It is impossible to tell how a finalist fared from the length of the break after the interview. Some Truman winners have left the panel speechless. Some finalists who were not successful have also left the panel speechless, albeit in a different way. Sometimes the panel is running late or is subject to external pressures (lunch delivery time, early flights).

Once we have interviewed every finalist from a state (the goal is to have a scholar from each state), there is usually a bit more time to discuss the finalists. This discussion may take place at the end of the day or during lunch, depending on the schedule. The discussion is sometimes over quickly, but more often it is wide-ranging, long, and bloody.

Oddly, the actual decision is usually the easy part. Most often, a clear Truman emerges from the fray. When no clear winner is apparent, we are often deciding among two or three frontrunners. The discussion can focus on many things: the student's performance in the interview, the written record, and the likelihood the candidate will go into public service. Any item in the application or in the interview is fair game for discussion and consideration.

The discussion does not focus, however, on the institution the student attends. Panelists do not consider the performance or the reputation of the school. The panelists do not know whether a school has other finalists in contention. The decision must be made based on the record of the finalist alone. The only time the school is discussed is in the context of what opportunities were available to the student.

In rare cases the panel may request a second interview. The second interviews happen at the end of the day and are very short, usually only a few questions. Second interviews are sometimes used when the panel cannot resolve a conflict without the input of the finalist, when the panel cannot determine which of two candidates should be selected as the scholar, or when a finalist freezes or breaks down during the interview. Finalists should not worry about second interviews, since they are so rare.

In order for a scholar to be named, the entire panel must agree. The foundation does not permit three-to-two votes. If the panel cannot come to an agreement, then that state might not have a scholar that year. Once a decision is made on each state, the panelists go through the same process to determine whether an at-large recommendation can be made. The at-large scholar can come from any of the states interviewed that day. Under normal circumstances, only especially large regions are guaranteed at-large scholars, but we do have the flexibility to award at-large scholarships in any region should a strong case be made. Scholars will never know if they are selected at-large, and the distinction between the state scholars and the at-large scholars vanishes as soon as the selection cycle is complete.

But what makes the difference between a Truman Finalist and a Truman Scholar? In the vast majority of interviews, the finalist did not say or do something wrong so much as the scholar said or did something right. Some candidates will have a day when their hair is perfect, the train is on time, the coffee shop gives them a discount for no reason, and they find a forgotten twenty-dollar bill in their pocket. Others will have one in which their shoelace rips, they arrive at the stop to watch the bus pull away, they drop everything they touch, including their coffee, and they find a forgotten leaky pen in a pocket. A million little things entirely outside anyone's control may impact a student's performance.

Even if a finalist attempts to control for luck—she shaves her head, sleeps at the interview site, forgoes coffee, and keeps pens only in little plastic baggies—she must now face the whims of the panelists. The panelists must negotiate their own interests and biases during the process. To account for bias, the Truman Foundation tends to gravitate toward lawyers and judges as panelists since they have practice putting aside their feelings. Although the panelists do an excellent job of putting aside their ideological, political, and personal beliefs, they still are people who ultimately make decisions based on who and what they like. One panelist's charming may be another person's smarmy; one panelist's delightfully restrained may be another panelist's off-puttingly aloof.

Although advisors cannot control the panel's perception of their candidates, they can control the information that we consider. In their letters of nomination, advisors should add context that helps the panel have the best possible interview with the student. If a finalist is slow to warm up, say that. If a student speaks slowly, let us know. We moderate our approach given what information is implicit in the application, but explicit information would help even more. At the very least, advisors should not oversell a finalist's personality in the letter of nomination. Quiet and thoughtful is fine—and is often a Truman—but not if we were told to expect a firecracker.

Preparation: Fight the Battle before It Begins

Much ink, bandwidth, and advisor brainpower has been spilled over how best to prepare students for an interview. The foundation sees countless different methods and levels of preparation. Panicked advisors contact the foundation convinced they are not doing enough or are doing too much. Given the variety of preparations made by different institutions, the best advisors can do is prepare their students enough but no more.

Although readers might shudder and demand to be told how many mock interviews to do, the level of preparation needed depends on the student. Some need more preparation just to be comfortable; some need less preparation so as not to appear artificial. By the time advisors (repeatedly) submit a student's materials, they should have some idea of the candidate's personality and comfort level with the interview process. Instincts about how much preparation a student needs are important to develop.

We recommend that students have at least one mock interview. The content of the mock interview is not nearly as important as just having the experience. Most students have not had the pleasure of having five slightly frightening, very impressive people peppering them with questions. Many students have not been asked to sit still in a suit for more than five minutes. Practicing both is a good way to prepare for the Truman.

When creating the mock interview, consider the tenor of the Truman interview. Interviews are rigorous—sometimes, they can even feel hostile—but they do tend to be conversational. The interactions between the panelists and the finalist are a bit more casual than some other interview settings. Truman panelists are sometimes intentionally funny. Train finalists how to read an interviewer for social clues. Students should know that it is okay to laugh at a joke or a lighthearted comment. They can relax into a conversational mode if that feels comfortable and seems appropriate. It is not a good idea for finalists to be more casual than the panel, but it is equally unwise to be much more formal. Good preparation helps students to understand how to negotiate this conundrum.

Covering logistics is helpful, too. Finalists often are anxious about things that seem silly but loom large as the stress of the interview draws near:

- *Does the dinner on the night before the interview count?* These dinners do not count, but they can help a finalist have a better interview. The panelists and the foundation's staff do not attend these dinners. They are organized and hosted by the Truman Scholars Association. The panelists do not receive a report from the dinners. Students who attend and meet fellow finalists, however, seem more at ease the next day.

- *Do I need to bring anything to the interview?* All students should bring identification. The panelists do not ask for original documents or additional materials. Finalists may wish to bring a copy of their application to review prior to their interview. Finalists should also bring something to entertain and distract them while they are waiting. A deck of cards is a good choice for the more gregarious and quaintly antique finalist; a laptop and headphones are an excellent choice for the more introverted.

- *Can I bring things into the interview room?* Finalists seem, for some reason, to want to bring things into the interview room. Generally, this practice is not recommended. Bringing additional items into the interview room seems to distract the finalist. Conversation grinds to a halt while a student jots down notes with a pad and a pen, or an overfull water bottle goes horribly awry. Things in the interview room also tend to distract the panel. One young lady insisted on bringing her overstuffed purse into the room, and several panelists could not stop staring at its bulging contents. She ultimately won, but she had to overcome her purse.

Students should surrender to the interview experience. The root cause of many unsuccessful Truman interviews has to do with students failing to demonstrate their personality, or any personality, during the interview. I doubt any advisor is telling students, "Go in there and be as dull as possible!" But sometimes that is what happens. Some of the lack of personality may be due to nerves, but some of it appears to be the result of a notion that being perfect is infinitely better than being interesting. We prefer finalists with texture—and flaws.

Too many mock interviews, or too much repetition of questions, tends to create a robotic response from the finalist. Finalists will fall madly in love with a turn of phrase and wedge it into conversation whenever possible. Varying the way questions are asked and discouraging students from relying on canned—or even partially canned—responses will help them avoid this trap.

Sharing the interview experiences of former finalists is fine, but exercise caution. The foundation knows that certain schools keep dossiers on questions we have asked and have extensive debriefs with those who have interviewed. This practice has not proven to be especially helpful. In some cases, students have become increasingly nervous when their information turned out to be inaccurate ("Wait. The panelists are being nice to me. I must really be doing a bad job! They hate me!"). Experiences are unique to that finalist at that time. Avoid relying on the experience of one person.

Likewise, gathering information about the panelists is not particularly useful, either. It is a good policy for the student to know who is going to be on their panel—members will be listed on the foundation's website.[5] All the information that the finalist is expected to know (name, title) can be found there. Finalists who obsessively google panelists in an effort to figure out how to woo them tend to come off as slightly creepy. The only exception would be if a student was interested in an issue that falls within the purview of one of the panelists. In that case, a bit of light research may be prudent. This research should be done only to avoid the very embarrassing moment when a finalist tries to condescendingly explain how a bill becomes a law while a professional hill staffer looks on.

The Aftermath: It's All Over but the Crying

I often tell the dramatic story of my own Truman interview. The story is compelling: a plucky working-class girl who wins over the hostile panel by her sheer charm and determination. The problem is that it did not happen that way. Louis Blair (the executive secretary of the Truman Foundation for sixteen years) was on my panel, and we have discussed this many times. His recollection, which is likely correct, can do nothing to change my impression. What I remember is what really happened, truth be damned.

Finalists often return with a story. There is usually a point where it all goes wrong—a wrong answer, a suddenly hateful panelist, or conspiring fates appear from nowhere to thwart the finalist's quest to be a Truman Scholar. But much like the apocryphal tale of my own interview, Truman interviews do not happen this way. Finalists do not lose a Truman over one unfortunate turn of phrase. Conversely, finalists do not win based on one clever turn of phrase—although one man came close.

This finalist was a clear frontrunner on paper: his public service commitment was outstanding; his leadership skills were exceptional; and he had a compelling personal story that cemented his future goals. Still his interview was unfulfilling. He seemed uncomfortable and reticent. After discussing all the finalists, we kept returning to him. We felt he was closest to the Truman Scholar selection criteria, but the interview left us with questions. We decided to call him back for a second interview and asked him one question, "If you could change anything about today, what would it be?" He said that he would like to stand up. He did; we conducted a second interview; and he won. Even in this case, he was the frontrunner. His defining moment merely cemented the Truman, but it did not win the day.

This story is one from thousands of interviews. The more typical but less dramatic story is one where a student's consistency wins over the panel. Finalists sometimes say truly unfortunate things during an interview; panelists sometimes let their attention wander; fire alarms sometimes go off midinterview; but a finalist cannot lose the scholarship based on one dramatic turn.

Of course, there are stories of panelists slamming shut their notebooks after a finalist answers a question carelessly and tales in which students were doing well until they revealed they were a Democrat or a Republican or a fan of Nickelback—and then it all turned sour. My favorite, which I hear every now and again, concerns a finalist who asked me, rather unpleasantly, to get her coffee. According to the story, she was doomed from the beginning. In truth, I thought her request was more funny than insulting, and I did not tell any of the panelists about it. Her performance in the interview was shaky, and she was not able to demonstrate her passion for service as compellingly as some of the other candidates. Her love of coffee never came up.

But the repetition of these stories is disconcerting. These stories place a lot of emphasis on details that matter little. Answering questions thoroughly is important; being polite is important; concealing a questionable taste in music is imperative; but one slip should not become the focus of the experience. Finalists should not turn the interview, which can be a valuable learning experience, into a referendum on this one moment.

In the inevitable postmortem, students should reframe the experience, thinking about what went well, what was enjoyable, and what they learned, keeping in mind that whatever the worst moment of the interview might have been, the panelists likely do not remember it. Sending thank-you notes helps diminish any lingering bad taste (like all of our panelists, I may not remember who answered a question poorly, but I do recall every thank-you note).

Regardless of the outcome, the foundation hopes that the Truman interview is a worthwhile experience. After each interview panel, we leave marveling at the number of high-quality applicants and lamenting the limited number of scholarships. The value of the interview is obvious to panelists: we are exposed to these wonderful applicants, and they are exposed to their fellow finalists. The foundation knows it cannot provide every deserving finalist with a scholarship, but we can at least introduce them to others who share their values. By understanding the nature of the interview, providing good preparation, and learning to manage the aftermath of the interview, faculty advisors can help to make sure the interview is a valuable learning experience.

10

An Advisor's Perspective on Reading Applications for Truman

PAULA WARRICK

An impressive feature of the Truman Scholarship program is its transparency with respect to the selection process. At the NAFA biennial meeting in 2013, deputy executive secretary Tara Yglesias led a simulation of the first round of the two-phase selection process. The goal of this process is to select around 165 finalists for the award, from which roughly sixty scholars will be chosen.[1]

In this same spirit of openness, the program invites experienced fellowships advisors to take part in the finalist selection process. The NAFA reviewers represent a subset of readers on the National Screening Committee (NSC) and are a combination of senior advisors from the Washington, DC, metropolitan area as well as past and present NAFA officers. I am both a DC-area advisor and a past president of NAFA, and I have been reading for Truman for five years. I am pleased to offer a description of the first-round selection process—albeit a subjective one—seen through the advisor's lens.[2]

How Applications Are Read

A remarkable aspect of the Truman selection process is how quickly the first-round screening takes place. In 2020, the Finalist Selection Committee (FSC) convened in Annapolis, Maryland, just nine days after the competition deadline. We were a twenty-three-person committee comprised of several different groups: the executive and deputy executive secretaries of the Truman Scholarship Foundation; midcareer public servants; professors and university administrators who work in admissions, career counseling, fellowships advising, and diversity initiatives; and a few longtime friends of the Truman program. Our collective expertise allows us to analyze the feasibility of applications from multiple angles. We can evaluate candidates' knowledge of and preparation for their proposed graduate studies, the suitability of their projected career pathways, and their understanding of the realities of their desired public service careers. As an advisor, I feel that I contribute empathy; having worked with eight dozen candidates over the years, I understand challenges that lead students to submit less-than-perfect applications. I should add that the committee is well-versed on the ethos of the Truman Scholarship. Many readers are longtime FSC members, and a good number of them are also Truman Scholars.

We work from Thursday through Saturday afternoon—right through Valentine's Day in 2020. We begin the selection process with a calibration exercise in which we compare our individual ratings of sample applications that we have read and scored in advance. Afterward, we break up into three-person teams and start reading. The teams are chaired by designated "box captains," so named for the boxes of applications they oversee. Box captains are especially seasoned readers who determine the order in which applications are read. They are knowledgeable about types of applications that can be challenging to interpret, such as those from students at military academies, which have unique institutional cultures. Box captains also talk us through rare instances when there are strong differences of opinion on an application's merits. They guide the pace of reading and ensure that we select an appropriate number of finalists from the files assigned to us.

We read applications according to the candidates' home states and regions. The sixteen regions correspond to the regional review panels listed on the Truman website.[3] Over the course of three days, each committee selects finalists for two or three regions. Regions consist of candidates from up to five states, but California, New York, and Texas are home to so many nominees that they are placed in two-state regions. Applications from Puerto Rico and sometimes other U.S. territories are often read separately.

We select about eleven finalists per region, but we have some leeway in determining the number of finalists for each state. If a state has fielded unusually strong candidates in that application cycle, we can modestly adjust the distribution of finalists across states within the region. Every effort is made, however, to achieve a balanced representation of state finalists. We are encouraged to identify at least one finalist per state, even though sparsely populated states field fewer applicants. If a state has no finalists after the initial screening, the box captain consults with Truman senior staff, who take a second look at the files. As soon as all finalists have been selected for a region, Truman program staff email them with good news about their status. Unsuccessful candidates are notified by email soon after the entire review process ends, no later than Monday, but often by late Saturday evening.

Each application is read by two committee members and scored according to a rubric (see Appendix B). The rating form allows us to award up to three points for various categories of excellence, including the overall public service record, leadership record, appropriateness for graduate study, and overall coherence and quality of the application. A nominee who shone in every one of these categories would earn twelve points. More than eight points is defined as "outstanding," while fewer than six points is "not a finalist." Readers adhere to the request to be tough graders. In my experience, few candidates receive outstanding ratings, and many nominees advance to the next round of competition with a score as low as six, which is classified as "good." Given the relatively narrow range of scores, one factor that can play a decisive role in a candidate's success is the bonus that we may award. We are permitted to increase applicants' scores by up to one point if they have shown great determination in pursuing their public service goals in the face of adversity. Because many nominees have overcome obstacles in life, this point is difficult to earn. As I have gained experience as a reader, I have awarded this point more sparingly.

As a reader, the most sobering aspect of the review process is the asymmetry between how long the applicants take to develop their applications and how quickly their files are scored. Each team is responsible for just over one hundred applications, allowing readers about fifteen minutes to assess each file. Candidates whose applications are clearly outstanding or weak either advance or are set aside with limited further discussion. Many applications fall somewhere in the middle, however, and readers debate their strengths and weaknesses in conversation. One strong point of the Truman evaluation process is that the reviewing is done in person, allowing space for thoughtful discussions rooted in readers' varied expertise. We learn from one another and sometimes change each other's minds when we differ over a candidate's merits.

A few guidelines to the committee are worth mentioning. We are asked to pay limited attention to the policy proposal unless the candidate meets the general criteria for advancement. Readers might skim proposals to make sure that the bibliography is solid and that the topic is logical. By "logical," I mean that it seems sensible and that it connects to Question 9, which asks students to describe the needs of society they wish to address in their public service careers. Additionally, our trainer (Tara Yglesias) reminds us that we are picking human beings, not well-written institutional endorsements, and that candidates must make their own cases for advancement in their application essays. Finally, we discuss criteria for evaluating nominees' choice of graduate degrees. The MBA is the only degree that is actively discouraged; however, degrees that could lead to lucrative jobs in the private sector, such as an MD or JD, also receive extra scrutiny. If a candidate proposes a dual degree, the added value of the second degree must be clear.

Reflections on Applicants

The Neoplatonic Ideal

Successful applications have an inner logic that allows readers to recognize a match between the ethos of the Truman Scholarship and our impression of the nominee as a future public servant. Various factors contribute to this level of coherence.

The candidate's vision and autobiographical trajectory. Readers should envision the nominee as someone who is poised to become a driving force behind a needed process of societal transformation or advancement. The ideal candidate can articulate a complex problem, has investigated the expertise needed to address it in the future, and demonstrates the preparation and force of personality needed to become an agent of change. To impress a harried reader in this way, candidates need to understand the interconnectedness of the essay questions and create obvious linkages. Their responses to Question 9 must connect to their activities lists, transcripts, proposed graduate training, responses to Question 8, and intended career paths. Most advisors help their applicants understand the architecture of the application, and with their institutional endorsement letters, they improve readers' ability to connect dots. In the weakest applications I read, however, the candidate fails to understand the intent behind Question 9 and selects a random topic, and/or the endorser does not provide a coherent introduction to the applicant.

Aptitude: A passion for public service and leadership potential. Reviewers must believe that candidates want to work in the public sector, despite its drawbacks. My next observation should come as no surprise, but some applicants project a more mature understanding than others of the nature of public service and the satisfaction it affords. Such depth of understanding can play an essential role in carrying a candidate through the entire application process, even when other aspects of the candidacy are less strong. Last year, through serving on a grand jury, I met a Truman Scholar who sometimes serves on regional interview committees. She observed that what often distinguishes scholars from finalists is simply their passion for public service. Her observation is valid for nominees who excel in the written phase of competition as well. There are a number of places on the application where candidates' commitment to the public welfare can shine through—in the coherence and clarity of their activities lists, or in their responses to Questions 8 ("Describe a particularly satisfying public service activity"), 9 ("Describe the problems or needs of society you want to address when you enter public service"), or 14 ("What additional information do you wish to share with the Truman Scholarship Foundation"?). In reading, I pay attention to whether the response to Question 9 is compelling and to the level of service the nominee has devoted to that issue. I also read Question 8 for evidence that the candidate has found value in making a public service contribution or gained perspective on the challenges of serving the public good. The most essential quality, however, is a vision of where public service is most needed. When all is said and done, candidates must stand for something. Having engaged in an impressive series of public service activities is, in and of itself, an insufficient basis for advancement.

Transformational leadership potential is another desired applicant quality. The strongest nominees possess a philosophy of change and understand the mechanics of power. The most obvious place to describe leadership is in Question 7, in which candidates discuss a specific example of their leadership. Some candidates make themselves memorable by knocking their responses to this prompt out of the park. More often, however, readers glean an appreciation of candidates' leadership by reading across their activities lists, essays, and letters. Here, as well, candidates' maturity plays an important role. Some nominees skillfully convey a personal philosophy of leadership, sense of responsibility toward others, or awareness of power dynamics.

Reality

In reality, of course, there are few perfect nominees—and this makes the process of evaluating applications intellectually engaging. Any number of problems can diminish a nominees' luster. As juniors, they may be just getting to know their majors. Their seamless pursuit of an academic and preprofessional trajectory may be disrupted by indecision or inexperience, a family or health emergency, or a study abroad experience with a fixed and not terribly relevant curriculum. Recommendations fall through or fail to capture the essence of candidates as we know them.

Candidates' approaches to their autobiographies can either help or hinder the process of developing their applications. Some nominees have good raw material for their essays because their life experience is intertwined with their goals in public service. If a nominee took on extra jobs in order to help a parent make monthly rent payments, it might be hard to question the authenticity of her desire to become an advocate for affordable housing. The nominee might not, however, want to reveal the source of her commitment to this topic. Life experience can be a detriment to the writing process when the privacy of a loved one is at stake or when the candidate is afraid to provide a glimpse of a chaotic family life. The resulting application can seem aloof, and gaps in the nominee's life trajectory may be unexplained. Readers understand that candidates face these challenges. We do our best to read across each application in search of evidence that the candidate meets the selection criteria.

Finally, nominees might attend institutions with limited histories of success in the Truman competition. Readers might lobby for such candidates, provided the essential selection criteria are met, if they feel that advancing them would build institutional understanding of the regional interview process. For this reason, it is appropriate for endorsements to mention a lack of institutional experience with the Truman competition.

Takeaways: Notes to Myself on How to Support Future Applicants

No matter how much guidance the Truman Foundation gives readers, an element of subjectivity is inherent to the review process. For this reason, I have written my advising take-aways from the review process as a series of reminders to myself.

Identifying Candidates

Moving forward, I will place less emphasis on the candidates' grades and more on their leadership and public service experience. In reading applications, I am surprised by how many nominees have near-perfect academic records. Readers are told that academic excellence is less important than applicants' leadership potential and a commitment to a career in public service. Though these three criteria are not mutually exclusive, advisors may be culling our nominees from an unnecessarily limited pool of prospective candidates. A better approach might be to focus on the relevance of applicants' curricula to their intended specializations in public service, or on nominees' efforts to acquire academic skills that are essential to their future public service endeavors.

Candidates with unusual interests or goals in public service stand out. During the campus selection process, I will remind my faculty committees to think broadly about the different manifestations of public service. When younger students confess that they have heard that the Truman program is only for political science or international relations majors, I will do my best to dispel this myth. I will tell them about Mara Menahan, a recent Truman Scholar who worked as in-house illustrator for the U.S. Botanic Garden, and I will also let them know that one of the longtime FSC members is a respected wildlife conservationist.

Mentoring Nominees

I will keep in mind the advice of a favorite mentor, a fellow art historian who was tapped to mentor her institution's Truman nominees because she won a series of university-wide teaching awards. She advised me to select one essay prompt for my students to answer first. Then, they should build their answers to each of the other questions around this central response. Her approach has helped me to convey to students that they need to develop a conceptual scaffolding for their applications. For my mentor, the anchor question was Question 8 (a satisfying public service activity). I prefer to begin with Question 9 (an issue or need in society), and to move on to the career and graduate school questions from there (first Questions 12 and 13, then 11 and 10, and finally the Washington Summer Institute question; see Appendix A).

I will develop a sixth sense for instances when my nominees' responses might sound like everyone else's. I will do this by staying up on current events and being mindful of hot topics in public service. Immigration, refugee policy, or voter suppression might be the subject of many public policy recommendations, or leadership or public service essays. I will press candidates who chose popular topics to try to demonstrate an unusual complexity of thought or maturity of interest in their subject matter. I will also keep in mind that many leadership essays are devoted to rehabilitating a dying club on campus, and that a great number of people want to go to law school. I will not automatically discourage nominees from writing about such subjects, however.

I will take special care with applicants who are obliged to write "Not Applicable" in their responses to Question 4 ("List government activities"). It is a red flag when a candidate can demonstrate no interest in politics or government, including campaign volunteering during election years. Nominees who lack material for this response should convey in their applications that they have been wholly devoted to other public service activities, as broadly defined in the Truman guidelines.

Advocating

I will do my best to ensure that my candidates' applications are bolstered by strong references. This includes my own endorsement, which will provide an overview of the nominee's goals in public service and commitment to a public service career. I will think of each endorsement letter as a portrait of a future public servant, and I will strive to quantify and contextualize this person's achievements. The authors of the leadership and public service letters will learn from me that they should confirm the details of the activities described in Questions 7 and 8 but go beyond this if they can. Why are these activities indicative of the nominee's suitability for an award that honors President Truman? If a seemingly strong candidate is not selected, I will make use of the appeals process. Readers are tough on applicants, on the grounds that such a process exists. If all else fails, and a candidate I believe in is turned down a second time, I will ask for feedback down the road, when the deputy executive secretary can offer it.

There is one thing I will not have to remind myself of, and that is the intent behind this feedback. For decades the Truman Foundation has committed itself to cultivating not just scholars, but advisors. In 1999, the University of Arkansas organized the first nationally competitive scholarship advising conference. Its goal was to help advisors to become more skilled in their advising of Truman and Marshall scholarship applicants. I recall going to that meeting just two days into my first advising position. I stood in line for some time, waiting for my turn to speak with a longtime Truman reader who was willing to walk me through my institution's most recent unsuccessful applications. I remember sweating a little and being humbled by the gap between his high standards and my own definition of excellent work. Twenty years on, it is still hard to meet those expectations.

11

You Sank My Fellowship
The "Near-Miss" Truman Application

TARA YGLESIAS

The foundation side of competitive fellowships has its frustrations. Well-meaning advice and instructions are ignored or, worse yet, interpreted in ways that strain both grammar and the space-time continuum.[1] Despite frequent warnings, absolutely everyone presses all the buttons on the application simultaneously at ten minutes to the deadline. Applicants thwart attempts to better understand their interests by offering platitudes and vague descriptions of already confusing campus activities.[2] And while the annoying jargon might change from year to year, the frustrations they generate maintain a nice, constant level of irritation.[3]

But much like any pool of Truman applicants, there is always an overachiever. For the past several years, that frustration has been the myth of the near-miss application. As fellowships advising has become more professionalized, there seems to be an increasing desire to treat competitive fellowship applications like puzzles rather than intellectual journeys. A quick scan of materials produced by members of the National Association of Fellowships Advisors (NAFA) includes myriad references to "cracking the code" and other phrasing that seems to suggest a Buzzfeed listicle rather than a sober pursuit of student growth.[4] Advisors become obsessed with the notion that if they just did *This One Thing* correctly, the outcome would be different. The application becomes a game, and too often advisors lose sight of both the application and the applicant as a whole.

There is a balance to be struck between "Top 10 Truman Must-Dos!" and an utterly holistic approach that considers the applicant's hopes and dreams but misses all the typos. This essay will explore the nuances of those applications that are close but ultimately not selected. While dispelling the myth of the near miss, this essay will discuss the reasons why close applications are not selected. Much of the essay will focus on the process of reading and how distinctions are made, but there will also be some discussion of areas of the application where issues often occur.

Jeopardy: What Is a "Near-Miss" Application?

Thanks to the increasing professionalization of advising, as well as the democratization of information on scholarships, applications are better prepared than ever. In the past decade, the number of wholly unsuitable applications has decreased to practically zero.[5] Instead the foundation has a few brilliant applications, a few not-so-brilliant applications, and the vast majority that reside in the middle. Their individual fates can be fickle indeed. Some of these applications will advance to finalist stage; the rest will not. The reasons why one application succeeds where another fails are often difficult to articulate and certainly do not lend themselves to a pithy article. But these applications are often where the disappointment is most acute and the feedback even more important. What was the undoing of the application? How can this be avoided in the future? What should we tell the student? If this student did not succeed, how can I expect success for any of my other students?

The Truman Foundation provides feedback to advisors on applications for those students not selected for interview.[6] There is a misconception that advisors spend the time arguing their student's case and contradicting the recommendations of the panel. In nearly every case, advisors tend to be able to spot the issues with an application at least as well as our readers. Only rarely does an advisor disagree totally with the reader's assessment. But a few do want to distill the criticism down to one specific item. Saying that "the student lacked leadership compared to the pool" is insufficient. These advisors will point to individual pieces of the application and try to debate the readers' findings. They want to know exactly when leadership is enough and the precise moment they failed to live up to the foundation's expectations.[7] Even those advisors who agree with our assessment often seem frustrated that we cannot point to the exact spot where the application went off the rails. These applications are what advisors consider near misses.

Providing feedback for these applications is often the most difficult. Improvements can always be made even in the applications of those selected as scholars.[8] But what should be improved is often unclear and sometimes subjective. There is never one slip that we can point to that is the difference between advancing and not. An applicant could follow every one of our #TrumanTips, an advisor could memorize every "Top 10 Truman Tips!" listicle, all the recommenders could avoid every common issue in letters of recommendation, and the application still might not be successful. These applications often fail to advance due to a mélange of choices the applicant made or larger issues involving the competitiveness of the pool.

For advisors, that explanation is often insufficient. In order to either assuage or justify the guilt of the participants, these applications must be distilled into *The One Thing* that was done wrong. General advice about the need for a compelling leadership essay gets translated into "do not write about student government." Suggestions for how best to present a case for a medical degree becomes "Truman does not fund medical degrees." The need to find something explicable—and be able to cast the blame elsewhere—is understandable. But continuing to treat the applications as if there are simple pitfalls to avoid leaves the student playing Application Whack-a-Mole: each time they are successful in removing an issue (not writing about medical school), another pops up (all of their service and academics are geared toward a degree in medicine). The end result is an application that ticks off the boxes but is denuded of any sense of what really drives the student. Even worse, the growth that the student could have from honestly completing the application is curtailed in an effort to avoid pitfalls.

Wheel of Application Misfortune

Truman applications are initially reviewed by a twenty-one-member Finalist Selection Committee (FSC). Applicants are grouped into regions by state of residence and given to teams for reading. Each three-person team spends an average of fifteen minutes per application. Every application is read twice; close or controversial applications are read three times.[9] Weak applications are removed, strong applications are advanced, and then the readers must deal with the vast majority of applications in the middle. Readers often have double or triple the number of close applications than they do spots for interviews. The difference between advancing and not advancing is slim.

There are three reasons why an application does not advance from the reading stage:

1. The Pool
2. Reader Malfunction
3. Application Malfunction

Readers are instructed to advance the top eleven candidates in each region. They are told explicitly not to consider:

- *State of residence.* The top applicants are advanced regardless of where they reside.
- *School affiliation.* Other than the general limit on nominations, there is no limit on how many students from a school can advance in the competition.
- *Subject matter.* Readers can advance as many applicants with the same topic as they wish.[10]
- *Degree program.* Other than a general prohibition against MBAs, the foundation does not set a degree-funding priority.

This list is not exhaustive, but these items are often suggested by advisors as reasons why their students do not advance. In reality, the reasons why some applications do not advance are more difficult to identify.

Go Fish: The Truman Applicant Pool

The applicant pool is the barrier to advancement for most applications. The difference in competitiveness of a region from one cycle to the next can be significant. One year's standout can be the next cycle's wallflower. More disconcertingly, it is nearly impossible to guess which regions might be most competitive in a given year. Given that students can generally apply from both their home address and their school address, it is even difficult to determine which institutions are likely to provide applicants in a given year.[11] Absent some sort of Godfather-esque vendetta against the other nominees, there is nothing to be done to dilute the strength of the pool. While increasingly infrequent, the foundation sometimes has applications that are in the wrong pool. Truman is often seen as a stepping-stone for other competitive fellowships. A student can be a good candidate for both Truman and another competitive fellowship, but there are also outstanding, compelling candidates who do not fit the Truman program—a student who has academic excellence and research experience, but little sense of how to translate that into compelling public policy, or a student who has leadership skills, but seems to lack an interest in public service. These students may score well in the evaluation process, but are ultimately not selected for interview because readers conclude they are "not a Truman." While this might suggest that advisors can identify these students early and not put them forward, the reality is quite different.[12] There is no way to tell what a pool looks like in a given year. The lone researcher or public service neophyte might merit an interview in a year when the pool is less strong.

In either case, the pool can keep an otherwise good candidate from advancing. Feedback will provide suggestions on ways to improve, but even if these suggestions had been followed, the application would likely not have advanced. Prevention is not an option. The best tactic to deal with the pool is both make sure the student is aware of the competitive nature of the application process and emphasize the growth that comes from diligently participating in the process. Even something as mundane as having a start on graduate school applications can be compelling for some students and provide some comfort if the pool keeps them from advancing. For the more evolved students, a focus on the growth that comes from exploring the ideas in the application itself can provide solace in the event the application does not advance.

Concentration: The Truman Application Reader

An infrequent, but still significant, cause of an application not advancing is reader malfunction. When tasking a human to do a lengthy, repetitive, yet subjective task that requires intense concentration but takes place amid plentiful food and warm ambient room temperatures, mistakes sometimes happen. Readers may give an application too little attention and miss the student's myriad achievements or give the application too much attention and be overly or unnecessarily critical. Sometimes applicants may be the unlucky victim of a shuffle that has their application being read immediately after the candidate who will go on to win Truman, Rhodes & Marshall, the MacArthur Genius Grant, and the Fields Medal before their eventual EGOT, and they suffer in comparison. It could happen that an applicant gets read immediately after something made the reader upset.[13] Even with their professional detachment, formidable stamina, and extensive training, readers are human. It is a subjective process. Hence each application is read by multiple humans.

Aside from the obvious advice of ensuring that the application is thoughtful and precise, the best way to control for reader error is through the appeals process. Schools are permitted to appeal one student not selected for interview to be reread by a second appeals committee. Information about the process is in the emails sent at the end of the selection cycle. Advisors are strongly encouraged to take advantage of the appeals process. The foundation's stated position is that any file is eligible for review on appeal. The foundation does not keep records of how frequently an institution requests appeals or the success rate of those appeals, so foregoing an appeal in an effort to save political capital for future years is not necessary. Additionally, it is virtually impossible for an advisor to be able to tell how close an application was to advancing, so a decision not to appeal might not be based on the best information. Appeals are not considered a second round of selection with lower expectations; these applicants are treated the same as any other once they are selected on appeal.[14] Students are not told of the appeals process unless they are selected for interview.[15] Some faculty have told their applicants about the process as a way to underscore that their application received thorough consideration. Focusing on this aspect may be helpful for some students while others might benefit from the finality of the process without discussing appeals.

Scattergories: Application Issues

Both a competitive pool and a potentially error-prone reader might be exacerbated by significant issues in the application. Significant is the key term in this case: these issues are not ones that can be corrected by adhering to a checklist.

Readers simply cannot determine when application issues are the result of a true lack of experience or an inability to effectively present those experiences. Readers are instructed to let the application make the case for itself—they are not to fill in blanks for students or give them the benefit of the doubt when responses are unclear.[16] While the sections below assume a deficiency in the application, several applications each year do not advance because applicants cannot effectively discuss their experiences.

The foundation encourages students to begin the Truman process early, in part because it helps position them for experiences necessary to be successful as a future public service leader, but also because students rarely have the ability to write well and present themselves clearly without a significant amount of time to review and reflect. Those who are serious about competitive fellowships and graduate school, particularly those students who come from backgrounds and majors where writing is not emphasized, need practice at establishing their voice. Even those students with robust writing backgrounds or innate skill need to unlearn academic writing in order to produce a more effective Truman application.[17]

Ticket to Ride: Establishing Leadership

Leadership is evaluated by considering the applicant's list of activities as well as their response to Question 7 ("a specific example of your leadership") and supporting letters.[18] Successful applications tend to exude leadership in other areas of the application as well, including in the service experience (Question 8) as well as the ambition in their career plans.

Truman has always had a somewhat nontraditional notion of leadership. Those students who merely occupy positions of authority, even impressive ones, are not necessarily leaders. Leaders are those who either take an existing leadership position and do something innovative with it or those who create their own leadership position around an issue of interest to them. As such, leadership experiences must be unique to the student. If any one of several students from a given organization could write the same essay, that probably means the student was not innovative with their leadership position. The foundation also tends to moderate what we expect from students based on what we know of the student's ambition and personality. Truman has different leadership requirements for students who lead through consensus in small-scale groups and plan for a career in that type of field than for students who express a desire to occupy a position of national leadership where controversy will be a daily occurrence.

With that leadership definition as a backdrop, there are three common issues in the leadership portion of the application. Each will come with an example of what readers see during the review.[19]

1. Guess Who? *"In weekly meetings, we planned a series of public events to make the issue more visible and to stimulate student interest. We developed and executed a detailed action plan, but I will share none of the details here. We did a lot of other things, perhaps individually, perhaps as a group. You will never know. I'm going to close without any data or clear indication of what anyone did individually."*

   Assuming it is not a nod to all things Truman, this issue of giving credit to others to the detriment of their own application seems to plague the Truman process.[20]

   This tendency is probably a function of what draws the applicants to service in the first place. While sharing credit is an admirable trait, it often leaves readers confused. Additionally, more and more organizations are eschewing traditional leadership structures, so it is doubly difficult to tell how much leadership is required of students if they will not explain themselves.

   Readers only have the student's words to understand and evaluate the activity, and readers are likely unfamiliar with the student's campus and only passingly familiar with their campus organization. Assuming that a reader will intuitively understand how important a role the applicant plays is risky. Applicants should be clear about their roles, the size of the student organization as well as its reach. This territory may be uncomfortable for students not used to basking in the limelight, but it is necessary for readers to understand the level of leadership involved.[21]

2. Apples to Apples: *"As a residence hall leader, I was responsible for answering student questions and organizing one information session a month. Once, I did one on recycling. In my mind, our campaign to*

raise awareness of recycling was a success. Yes, I know I had a very interesting internship listed in Question 4 that probably had a better leadership example in it. No, I'm not going to talk much about it."

Readers usually do not find campus enrichment activities— Model UN, debate, and, to a lesser extent, residence hall leadership, and student government—very compelling unless there is substantial leadership that is likely to translate into real-world skills. Engaging a captive audience of dorm room dwellers on campus issues is not nearly as impressive as shepherding that group through a time of controversy or crisis. That is not to say each leadership example needs to hinge on dramatic events, but it is helpful if there is a narrative arc of sorts. "I did a good job as SGA president" is not a narrative arc.

The problem with these activities is that they can be very, very time-consuming, but often do not serve to do much other than enrich the applicant's skill set. These sorts of activities often engage an already engaged group of students around an activity that is necessarily closed to other people. If students can find a way to use a campus organization to reach out to others beyond the organization or create change around an issue for a greater good, it is perfectly appropriate for a leadership essay. Unfortunately, the bulk of essays around such activities do not meet these criteria.

Emphasizing the service to others might be helpful. Most applications have leadership examples that reach beyond a small campus group. In comparison, a student whose sole leadership involves successfully shepherding their debate team can seem more self-serving and will not be as compelling. Having students look at the application as early as possible allows them to get an idea of where their application might be lacking.[22]

Interestingly, students often have other items in their applications that would prove more compelling. Just because an activity is time-consuming does not make it the best leadership example. Additionally, difficulty in getting a supporting letter is not a reason not to write about a leadership activity. A supporting letter is nice, but a letter that just mentions the activity can be perfectly acceptable. But please interpret this advice as narrowly as possible.

Finally, there really is no hierarchy of leadership activities. But readers often give feedback that draws a distinction between those activities they find compelling—where an applicant's organization, no matter how small or how specific an issue area, leads people on campus or in the community—and those they do not, where an applicant manages to organize a group of people already involved in an activity to improve things for themselves.

3. Connect Four: *"Please allow me to shoehorn in an activity from high school that I would like to mention. You will emerge confused as to the time frame of those efforts and what my current interests are."*

Readers put far greater stock in recent activities. An upward trend in leadership and service is often rewarded with an interview. But sometimes applicants, particularly nontraditional students, have significant leadership from before college. For those students it can be a struggle to present those items well in the application.

In general, overstuffing Question 7 is not the best way to ensure readers credit earlier leadership. If the leadership example is ongoing (perhaps the student started an organization in high school that they continue to lead), then the essay can have a longer-term focus. But in that case, students need to be clear about the timeline and to focus the essay on recent events even if there is more compelling leadership in the past. Those experiences can be discussed in detail in either the supporting letter of recommendation or in Question 14 (additional information).

Likewise, applicants who have several leadership activities around the same issue sometimes try to include all relevant experiences in one essay. Providing the readers with sufficient detail for more than one activity is nearly impossible given the space constraints of this essay. Readers want to see the applicant's leadership in detail on one specific issue. The overview belongs in the letter of recommendation.

Chutes and Ladders: Power Dynamics in the Truman Application

The Nominee Rating Form contains the rather dry phrase "appropriateness for proposed graduate study."[23] While that category includes the only reference to the transcript, the main purpose is to evaluate how the applicant understands power.[24] Readers will still sometimes refer to this characteristic as an applicant's "change agent potential," but business schools seem to have co-opted that phrase beyond all meaning.

Power in the Truman application is both about how the applicant plans to accumulate power and what they plan to do with power once they have it. Both components need to be in evidence for a successful application. Leadership, as described above, goes a long way to establishing that the applicant understands how to gain power. But the readers also need to see a clear plan for the next steps.

After applicants have established their areas of interest, the readers then look to their graduate school plans (Question 11) as well as their career goals (Question 12 for immediate employment after graduate school, Question 13 for five to seven years later) to see if the applicants have an understanding for how best to gather power in their chosen area. The applicant should show both an understanding of the needed academic credentials and the role intangible elements like network building, institutional prestige, and early career development opportunities play in the development of a power base.

From there, readers look to see what applicants plan to do with the power they have accumulated. It is not enough for an applicant to build an impressive resume; they need to also show that they plan to make a difference beyond burnishing their credentials. Readers look to Questions 12 and 13 to see not only a trajectory of leadership, but also a plan for change. The evaluation of these responses is very dependent on the applicant's interests as the reader understands them. It is important both that applicants clearly explain their interests and that their understanding of power is level with those interests. So an applicant with mostly local political involvement would be expected to accumulate and expend power in different ways from someone who aspires to being a player on the international stage.

But much like taking sole credit for leadership opportunities, Truman applicants also struggle to admit to their own ambitions. Convincing applicants that it is okay to admit to being ambitious can be a significant step forward. But the power dynamics of the Truman application can bump up against all sorts of other issues—imposter syndrome, a lack of quality mentoring, writing difficulties—so that it becomes imperative that the applicant at least accepts that power is a concept worth embracing. From there, applicants can work on mastering how they express their need for and use of power.

Mystery Date: *"Harvard, the most prestigious graduate school in the country, is my choice for a law degree. Please allow me to tediously list the required coursework." or "I plan to work for the Department of Justice in the Office of Extremely Long Names That Actually Don't Provide Much Information and Federal Programs. I shall provide no other information as to my ambitions."*

The purpose of Questions 12 and 13 is to get a better understanding of students' ambitions and determine if they have a clear idea of how best to impact the issues that concern them. While part of that includes a clear statement of which graduate school is best for them and where they would like to work, an extremely detailed view of either is unnecessary. The readers know a great deal about both graduate schools and public service career paths. Telling them that contracts is a required first-year course for law students does not come as a revelation. What does prove to be revelatory is an understanding of how applicants will transition from the graduate school plan of their choice to their first career. The applicant's ambition and understanding of their own skills is on display here. For some students, this section can reveal gaps in their knowledge or a misunderstanding of the skills needed to work on an issue. For others, it can reveal a lack of confidence in their own abilities.

Applicants should understand that these questions are not about who comes up with the best plan, but instead what is the best plan for them. Winning applications have proposed attending the top graduate school programs as well as programs that are relatively unknown. Some applicants propose getting right into the fray, while others are content with more measured growth. But for successful applicants, these questions reveal applicants' understanding of how best to credential themselves and then position themselves to have an impact.

Advising matters. The difference between an applicant who has access to good advising and those who do not is often marked. Encourage applicants to talk to people in the field other than professors. Aside from providing good practice in talking to adults, it will give applicants more career trajectories to choose from as well as the confidence to write about the path they have chosen.

1. Stratego: *"After five to seven years of working on behalf of the Department of State, I hope to be promoted to the Next Level of Bureaucracy. That is all. Thank you."*

Fortunately for the country, countless applicants each year want to dedicate their service to the bureaucratic institutions that probably contribute to the very problems they wish to address. Unfortunately for their applications, this dedication often makes for an unsatisfying essay.

Readers still expect to see leadership and an understanding of how change is made even when a student plans to work within an existing system that may be resistant to change. Applicants in these professions need to make a point of acknowledging the difficulties they will face, lest they appear naive. Speaking with someone in the field may prove helpful if only to assure the applicant that change is still possible.

Most applicants will not have a lot of space to discuss their understanding of the power dynamics in their bureaucracy of choice, but they should likely temper their stated ambitions to be appropriate to the office. Applicants may also choose to write a policy proposal for the same agency and thus have more room to display their understanding of the political nuances of working for an entrenched bureaucracy. Letters of recommendation can be very helpful in this area. Recommenders who are familiar with the institutions the applicant plans to work with can provide needed context.

2. Clue: *"I realize at no point have I mentioned an interest in children, which is why I plan a career in K–12 education."*

With the fixation on near misses comes a tendency to focus on parts of the application rather than the whole of the application. Each essay might be a work of persuasive genius but may still not give an overall picture of the applicant. At a minimum, the application reads as a disjointed series of accomplishments. But more often, it appears that the applicant does not understand the importance of experience.

These types of applications generally fall into two specific categories. The first is areas of interest where it is difficult to have relevant experience, particularly depending on the location of the applicant's institution. Applicants at a small liberal arts college in the Midwest may have a difficult time gaining direct, relevant experience in security or intelligence issues, for instance. But even in those cases, there are activities that relate to applicants' career goals that would allow them to demonstrate an understanding about how to have an impact on the issues of concern to them. The experiences can be classroom-based, in a related field, or through internships. For areas where direct experience is impossible, the application becomes about the student's persistence and understanding that experience is an important component of gathering power.

The other category is experience that should be fairly easy to come by, but, for whatever reason, an applicant chooses not to gain that experience. This situation occurs most often in two areas: education and poverty. Readers tend to react negatively to those applicants who plan a career in poverty research without ever seeming to have met poor people, or those who plan to revamp education policy without ever having been around children. Convincing readers that an interest is sincerely held is difficult when an applicant cannot be bothered to have at least some experience in the two most abundant types of campus service activities available. Applicants should demonstrate that, in addition to their formidable intellect, they have an understanding of the human components of their issue.

In both instances, applicants should take care not to frame their experiences narrowly. A campus activity that requires discretion and consensus building on the part of applicants can demonstrate that they have the capability to work in a sensitive field like intelligence. Likewise, a volunteer program with school-aged children can demonstrate that an applicant is more than a heartless, number-crunching bureaucrat. Applicants can use Question 8 (a significant public service experience) to tease out these connections and provide the reader with the assurance that they understand the power dynamics of their issue.

3. Dominion: *"I plan to run for office because I believe that to whom much is given, much is required. When I am elected, I plan to ensure that we are a nation of laws, solving a variety of social ills. I will now communicate my plan in vague phrases."*

There are certain applicants who inherently understand power. They have accumulated power since arriving on campus and often use it for good. But they can lack a clear vision of how to use that power. These applications are usually marked by a feeling that applicants are being buffeted from one issue to another, the only connection being that it was a place where they had power and could exert it.

Applicants who struggle to write Question 9 (describe a problem or need of society you want to address) often fall into this category. Their responses to Question 9 are often vague in telltale ways, relying on hoary phrasing and general discussions of issues like civil rights or inequality. These applicants may also struggle with Questions 11 (graduate school) and 12 (career immediately following graduate school) because they are focused on the end goal of elected office.

That is not to say these applicants are not appropriate for Truman. But they do require a check on their heretofore unchecked power. Not that the worry is a turn to public service despotism, but an application that displays an understanding of power but does not demonstrate any relevant values ensures the applicant will seem a cipher to readers.

For these applicants, a little soul-searching is in order. They need to reflect on why they are interested in accumulating power, and how they have used it in the past. Generally, there is some issue in which they are most engaged. That issue may be as vague as "political engagement," but at least that is a possible foundation for the application. These applications often benefit from reads by people who do not know them or their work well. Such readers can often point out when applicants have become a bundle of ambition versus when they are conveying their values as well as their understanding of power.

The Game of Life: Bringing the Application Together

Perhaps the reason why those "Top 10 Truman Tips" lists are so appealing is that they make pulling the application together seem easy. Just check for these few items, make sure public always has an "L" in it, and success is guaranteed! The reality is much more nuanced.

Advisors will never be able to control the strength of the pool in a given cycle. Advisors will never be able to ensure every application reader is well fed and cheerful when they read an application. Advisors cannot fix a student who writes imprecisely or refuses to put in the necessary time to make a successful application. Advisors cannot will a student to have the necessary leadership to advance or the understanding of power to make their application stand out. Even if an advisor identifies a problem with an application and the applicant is inclined to fix it, most of these issues cannot be sorted with a quick redraft.

But what advisors can do is use the application as a tool. Early identification of potential applicants means they will have more time to develop leadership skills and understand the realm in which they want to make a difference. It also means that the applicants can have more conversations about the work they love, and that can lead to internships, volunteer experiences, jobs, and other new opportunities. Applicants can take the time to improve their writing, something that will pay dividends throughout their careers. For many applicants, even those not selected for interview, the process of the Truman application is transformative in determining their path in public service. Applicants think not just about the end goal but how to get there and what experiences to have along the way.

It is not easy abandoning the notion that these applications are games to be won, and that readers can be defeated with the right assortment of tips and cheat codes.[25] But moving away from the "near miss" and toward a holistic view of the application makes for both better applications and more enriched applicants. And that is a Yahtzee.

Part III

Why Does It Matter?

12

The Truman Scholarship
Having a Winner Every Time

LOUIS H. BLAIR

For sixteen years, I served as the director of a program that granted more than two million dollars in scholarship assistance each year. The Truman Scholarship Foundation touched lives in various ways, serving students well beyond the money it awarded. I found the work as rewarding as any in my career because of this support to students throughout the process and beyond it. The broad value of the program was clear in the many warm letters I received. The most satisfying ones were those that came from persons who were not selected as Truman Scholars, but who recognized themselves as winners nonetheless.

The following is from a Truman contestant, passed on by the faculty representative of an institution that had never had a Truman Scholar at the time and rarely had a Truman finalist, but frequently had participants in the Truman competition.

> As you may know, Tuesday the finalists for the Truman Scholarship were posted. Unfortunately, I did not make it to the interview round. You are right; the finalists look like tough competition!
> I just wanted to thank you for giving me the opportunity to try for this scholarship. There is no disappointment in not making it, when you give it your best shot and learn something in the process. This has

been a learning experience, in that I see where I am, what things I need to improve, and long-term goals I need to set. I'm constantly on the lookout, now, for new ways to get involved in my career interests, understand what I truly want for myself in the future, and how this can be accomplished.

Thank you so much for all the time you have spent helping me. You've been absolutely wonderful. When professors whom I respect show such support and encouragement for my future it makes me realize I sometimes underestimate my ability, and that is perhaps the only thing holding me back. Your enthusiasm has created quite a positive difference in my attitude and in my life and I want you to know how much that is appreciated!

—A Truman candidate

While I received relatively few letters of such careful construction and such gracious appreciation, I received a dozen or more each year sharing similar sentiments. I also heard often from Truman faculty representatives that they too received warm notes of gratitude.

General Benefits of the Truman Application Process

The foundation conducted many surveys during my time as executive secretary there. I have a program evaluation background, largely from having spent more than a decade conducting assessments of public programs as a staff member at the Urban Institute and at two organizations whose responsibilities were to assess the performance of government programs. I believe in conducting surveys to get objective opinions from clients on how well they feel government programs have served them. The Truman Foundation was pleased to provide Dr. Larkin Dudley of the Center for Public Administration and Policy at Virginia Tech a grant to conduct follow-up interviews with unsuccessful Truman candidates. Her charge was to conduct twenty- to thirty-minute structured telephone interviews with Truman candidates one year after they had submitted an application and not been selected for a Truman and to find out what they thought about the experience. Roughly half of the candidates surveyed had not been invited for a Truman interview although they had clearly worked hard on their applications.

The bottom line question was the following:

Question: "Thinking about your experience with the Truman
Scholarship, are you satisfied that you applied for a Truman
Scholarship even though you were not selected?"
Responses [N=127]:

Very satisfied	67 percent
Somewhat satisfied	24 percent
In effect, "Wish I had never heard of the Truman Scholarship Foundation"	9 percent

These results were consistent with the findings of recent surveys.
Every year, the Truman Foundation surveys candidates who reach the
interview stage. For this particular project, Dr. Larkin surveyed 221 finalists at the end of the day of their interview. All finalists reported one or
more substantial benefits from the application process, the most frequently
mentioned being that the process:

Clarified my career goals and objectives	82 percent
Gave me a better understanding of my policy topic	75 percent
Helped me begin serious planning for graduate school	64 percent
Made me more aware of my values and interests	63 percent

General satisfaction with the Truman application and interview
process:

Very satisfied	73 percent
Somewhat satisfied	26 percent
Generally dissatisfied	1 percent

The Truman Scholarship application was designed to be a structured
diagnostic tool to help students think about what is important to them
and to get them to begin planning for their post-baccalaureate careers in
terms of graduate education and work before and after graduate education.

Careful, sustained effort is required to put together a credible
application. Students who devote extensive amounts of time to an
academic exercise with faculty supervision and guidance should grow in
maturity.

What are some ways that Truman representatives can make Truman applicants winners every time even if not all will actually receive the scholarship or even an interview for the scholarship? They should sell the program appropriately during the recruitment of candidates, and let them know such things as:

What winning means. The odds of being selected as a Truman Scholar are long: typically there are seven hundred applicants and only sixty-five scholars selected. Winning does not mean only being selected as a Truman Scholar. Winning includes:

- Learning about themselves through the process
- Gaining better presentation skills
- Making suitably ambitious plans for the future
- Getting prepared for applications in the senior year, for other post-baccalaureate fellowships, or for admission to competitive graduate schools

A substantial amount of work is required to prepare a good application. Candidates who advance to the interview phase of the Truman competition frequently spend as much time on the Truman process as they spend on a three-hour demanding course.

Advisors and other faculty will be there to help and encourage them along the way. The Truman application requires a great deal of introspection and extreme care in answering the questions and presenting the material. Many students will not be used to doing such work. Candidates often get bogged down or discouraged.

Truman candidates are being honored by representing the university. Advisors believe that nominees have the values, experiences, intellect, and persona to proudly represent their institutions before a panel likely to include a United States Court of Appeals judge (one step removed from the U.S. Supreme Court), one or two university or college presidents, a leader in the public service, and a former Truman Scholar on a fast track to prominence in the public service.

Understand What the Truman Foundation Is Seeking in Terms of Candidates and Written Materials

While useful for all involved, the process is likely more satisfying in the long run for advisors who work with the types of candidates the foundation seeks and if they understand what parts of the application are most critical in the review.

What does the foundation seek? It seeks people who are intent upon becoming change agents to improve the operations of government agencies and to establish or enhance the operations of existing nonprofit and advocacy groups that either serve people (especially those in need of assistance) or protect resources. The foundation has no preferences as to whether scholars aspire to work at the local level or the national level, in the United States or abroad, in low-profile or high-profile positions. It does care that the bottom line for the student is service and improvement of conditions for others. This has always been an essential tenet of the program (before, while, and after I served as its executive secretary).

There are two types of students advisors should give attention to recruiting:

1. Outspoken advocates full of passion, piss, and vinegar who could lead a movement for change, perhaps taking on entrenched interests on behalf of causes in which they believe and having some chance to make a difference.
2. Exceptional students who work well with administrators or faculty and could have some influence. Those who are competitive for awards like the Truman Scholarship often serve as a student trustee of the university or student member of a presidential or dean search committee.

The Truman selection process is not grades-driven. The foundation's selection panels care far more about the quality of the candidates' public service record and ability to bring about change than about grades. The foundation does care that the Truman Scholars will be good students in whatever graduate program they attend, but the foundation is not giving priority to people who will become editors of the law review or otherwise first in their graduate school class. Advisors who do not have a good sense of what the foundation seeks should review http://www.truman.gov and browse around. If this exploration raises specific questions, contact the foundation at office@truman.gov.

Make clear to students expectations for success. These are likely to be their serious commitment to the application, willingness to consider advice and constructive criticisms that advisors and other faculty/staff offer, submission of a good product that reflects favorably on the student and on the institution, openness to growth during the process, and graciousness in thanking all of the persons who worked on their behalf.

Be accessible to candidates. Successful Truman candidates (i.e., those who put together polished applications and have sufficient credentials to get to a Truman interview) will spend up to one hundred or more hours on their Truman applications and policy proposals. They will need encouragement to keep going and help in refining drafts. Often, a few weeks before the deadline, candidates reach a stage of high anxiety—referees have not provided letters, responding to Question 14 is difficult, they cannot get the policy recommendation onto one page, and similar types of complaints. They need guidance and reassurance.

Advisors need to be there for them, recognizing that this can require a significant time commitment. A Truman representative who is vice president for student affairs at a California university once said to me:

> Louis, I have some bad news and some good news. First the bad news, we have no Truman nominees this year. The good news is that I was able to get my work done for the university in the month leading up to the Truman deadline.

While this might be a bit of an exaggeration, the application process is time consuming for the candidate and for the faculty representative.

Find ways for the institution to recognize the candidates, regardless of the outcome. Recognition can come in a number of ways, such as: dinner with the president of the institution for all nominees for major scholarships regardless of the outcome, a specially selected book with a personal inscription from a faculty member, modest funding for a senior thesis or a summer travel grant, and academic credit for having gone through the process.

Put the Truman outcome in perspective. This is not a life or death outcome. While winning can increase the speed with which these future change agents attain their goals and ambitions, failure to come home with the Truman should not affect a student's ability to get into and find a way to cover the costs of a first-class graduate institution, nor will it diminish the likelihood of achieving long-term goals.

Every year, talented Truman applicants who were not successful go on to achieve success and distinction in other highly competitive scholarship programs. Sometimes they are not exactly who the Truman seeks to reward but they are who the Rhodes, Marshall, Mitchell, or other programs seek. Sometimes the candidate has not put together a stellar application or a compelling interview for the Truman, but does so for scholarships a year later. Typically a dozen unsuccessful Truman applicants each year will be selected in subsequent years for a Rhodes, Marshall, Mitchell, Gates, Schwarzman, and any number of other awards.

Encourage the students to use the process to build for the future. Little if any of the work that goes into the Truman application is wasted, even for persons not selected. The response to Question 14 ("What additional information would you like to provide?") can be the basis for a personal statement for a post-baccalaureate fellowship. Responses to other requests for information on the application (such as "describe one specific example of your leadership," "describe a recent particularly satisfying public service activity," "describe the problem or need of society you want to address when you enter public service," "describe the graduate program you intend to pursue if you receive a Truman Scholarship," "what do you hope to do and what position do you hope to have upon completing your graduate studies?") should provide much of the structure for applications to graduate school. Answers to these questions, along with the response to the policy proposal, should help candidates determine the type of graduate school education most appropriate for them.

Advisors cannot guarantee the selection of their candidates as a Truman Scholar, no matter how strong or how well they meet the criteria above. By understanding the Truman program and following this plan with an engaged, dedicated candidate, advisors can guarantee nominees a winning experience in the Truman Scholarship competition.

13

Giving Shape to a Future Career Path through the Truman Process

JANE MORRIS AND ELIZABETH VARDAMAN

Founded with a mission to democratize the process of applying for nationally competitive scholarships, the National Association of Fellowships Advisors (NAFA) traces its roots to conferences organized in the 1990s by the Truman Foundation. Those initiatives were designed not only to encourage increased numbers of scholarship advisors to become fully informed about the nature of and goals for the Truman Scholarship, but also to promote the broad benefits for students engaging intensely with the application process.

The Truman-Marshall conference held in Fayetteville, Arkansas in 1999 became the lodestar from which the guiding principles for NAFA emerged and took their first light. Mary Tolar, then the deputy executive secretary of the Truman Foundation and now the director of the Staley School of Leadership Studies at Kansas State University, provided the overarching vision for a professional organization of scholarship advisors. Suzanne McCray provided the venue and many of the resources. Within a year after the Fayetteville conference, a small band of scholarship advisors from across the U.S., under leadership from Mary Tolar, Robert Graalman, Beth Powers, and Jane Curlin, among others, took first steps toward establishing a national scholarship organization. From its inception, NAFA was deeply intertwined with the Truman Foundation and shared its core conviction of the innate value of the scholarship application process.[1]

The Pedagogy of High-Impact Practices and Scholarship Advising

The pedagogy that underscores the value of the process promoted by the Truman Foundation derives from education research exploring the connections between self-reflection and learning that dates back to 1910 and the writings of John Dewey.[2] In his seminal work, *How We Think*, Dewey examines the process by which learners, faced with perplexing observations, reflect as they test hypotheses to form conclusions based upon prior knowledge and experiences:

> Reflection involves not simply a sequence of ideas, but a consequence—a consecutive ordering in such a way that each determines the next as its proper outcome, while each in turn leans back on its predecessors.[3]

More recently, research on the impact of self-reflection in higher education has transformed teaching and learning in colleges and universities, leading organizations such as the Association of American Colleges and Universities (AAC&U) to promote High-Impact Practices (HIP) as educational tools that engage students more deeply in the learning process.[4] Implementation of HIPs such as first-year seminars, common intellectual experiences, global study, and service learning has proven effective in supporting learning outcomes and beneficial to students from diverse backgrounds. Much has been written and discussed in NAFA circles about the impact of such practices for student applicants apart from or in addition to the scholarship outcomes. The tables of contents in NAFA proceedings are replete with articles demonstrating the connections between scholarship advising and HIPs such as undergraduate research, study abroad, and reflective writing. Importantly, the growth of the scholarship advising profession suggests that applying for nationally competitive scholarships has in itself become a HIP, driving transformation within our institutions and providing greater access to these opportunities for all students.

In *All Before Them: Expanding Access through Nationally Competitive Awards* (2015), Karen Weber, Executive Director of Duke's Office of Undergraduate Scholars and Fellows (OUSF), wrote about her experience with e-portfolios when she was the associate dean of the honors college at the University of Houston. Initially, she expanded e-portfolio use for scholarship applicants, then expanded this practice more broadly within the honors college, and ultimately to other programs within the University.[5]

The unifying principle that connects HIPs—scholarship advising in particular—to successful student outcomes is the practice of active self-reflection that guides students through the challenges of developing an academic and cocurricular undergraduate path that leads to postgraduate lives where they can make meaningful contributions to society. The act of writing a compelling scholarship application with the advice and support of faculty and scholarship advisors allows student applicants to step back from all of their coursework and activities in order to connect them to the goals of the scholarship program and more broadly to their long-term goals.

The extraordinary value of scholarship application processes and mentorship is one of the pillars on which in 2001 Richard Light built a groundbreaking case in *Making the Most of College: Students Speak Their Minds*.[6] The sixteen hundred interviews the book is based on provide insights on how students connect knowledge gained through lived experiences with their academic studies. Among those Light interviewed, thirty were Rhodes and Marshall Scholars. Light reported that an important theme across these applications was that "at key points in their college years an academic advisor asked questions, or posed a challenge, that forced them to think about the relationship of their academic work to their personal lives."[7] Such testaments are compelling evidence that buttress John Dewey's philosophy of reflective learning. As a tool for academic and career advising, scholarship applications can be valuable in helping students choose courses and majors as well as helping them decide how to use their time outside of the classroom. This article will explore how the Truman Scholarship application, in particular, is a tool for active self-reflection that can help undergraduate students as early as their first year to choose wisely and engage deeply.

So Many Applications—Why Truman?

Scholarship applications run the gamut from the one long essay in which Rhodes Scholarship applicants write about their motivations, credentials, and goals for changing the world through postgraduate study at Oxford to the 150-word eight-improbable-facts prompt in the Knight-Hennessy Scholarship process. Applications for the Goldwater Scholarship and the Udall Scholarship (both of which were established after the Truman Scholarship) resemble the Truman application but modified to determine the applicant's fit for becoming a research scientist, tribal health or policy advocate, or environmental change agent. Postgraduate scholarship applications assess applicants at the end—or sometimes after—their undergraduate studies. Academic and extracurricular choices have been made, internships and research experiences completed, study abroad done. Such assessments make sense in a world where all applicants have access to the same level of opportunity and advising. They assume that all applicants enter college knowing exactly who they are, where they will go after college, and how they are going to get there. The real world is a bit different than that.

The Truman Scholarship application was significantly enhanced in the late 1980s by Louis Blair, when he assumed the reins as executive secretary of the Harry S. Truman Scholarship Foundation.[8] Mary Tolar remembers well that time when Mr. Blair (as he was affectionately called by Truman Scholars) redesigned and enhanced the application process: "For years, students applied for the Truman Scholarship as sophomores. From the start, the application was intended to not only identify interested students, but to help them explore public service as a career. When Louis Blair became executive secretary, he introduced changes to the application and to the process that moved candidates beyond exploration to preparation and commitment. Juniors now apply. The policy proposal component replaced a less structured essay prompt. Students interested in public service are guided with intention to prepare for graduate study and commit with confidence to a public service career. The process certainly serves the student, and at a critical point in their college experience. It also serves the future of public service leadership that the Truman Foundation was founded to support and promote. (Everyone wins!)."[9]

The application breaks down a personal statement into sections that move applicants from their extracurricular activities to choices about their academic paths to visions and plans for futures in which they serve the public and change the world. The application begins with questions about the applicant's demographics and academics—where the applicant lives, where they go to school, their major, GPA, and so on, as well as their intended postgraduate degree. This basic information helps in the review process mainly to establish eligibility and the geographic region in which the application will be reviewed. The heart of the application begins with Questions 1–6, and though they appear to be mostly résumé-like questions, they actually reveal a great deal about the applicants' trajectory since high school and the ways they are investing personal time beyond the classroom. What prompts applicants to reflect on these activities are the categories into which they fall and the judgment of the applicants, who are asked to list them in order of priority. Deeper reflection in Questions 7–9 about leadership, public service, and society's most pressing issues requires applicants not only to assess the world around them, but also to place themselves into that world as agents for change. These questions in particular help students start to understand their own values and prompt them to think about ways in which they can become difference-makers and meaningfully affect their future professional realms.

As tools for active self-reflection, Questions 10 and 11 focus on the academic choices that applicants have made and will be making. In discussing their top three classes taken to date, junior-level applicants must consider which of the twenty or more classes they have taken are the most relevant to their long-term plans. While students in their first or second year may not yet have that perspective, a question about course choices in the context of where a student might want to be after college can be helpful in thinking about their choice of major. Question 11 probes the candidate's thoughts about postgraduate study as a Truman Scholar. Not all students will pursue postgraduate studies, but many will. Asking students early in their undergraduate studies about graduate or professional school can give them the opportunity to weigh the value added to their careers and encourage them to explore majors that will prepare them for graduate education. Such consideration would be beneficial even for students who have no plans to study beyond their undergraduate education. This process helps students discern what is important and necessary to them, and what is not.

Reporting on short-term and longer-term plans in Questions 12 and 13 allows students to think strategically and realistically about where their education will place them professionally in anticipation of their impact on the issues they raised in Question 9. Having students consider how they might move from entry-level positions to a career has value well beyond that of the Truman Scholarship itself. In imagining a realistic career path at this point in the application, a student *reflects* on the responses to all the prior questions and decides what makes sense and is most appealing to them as they move forward. Such a process fits precisely with Dewey's definition of self-reflection as a "consecutive ordering in such a way that each determines the next as its proper outcome, while each in turn leans back on its predecessors."[10] These facets of the Truman process have inspired some directors of academic programming to create whole introductory courses. Oklahoma State University's "Windows on the World" is an example of a one-hour honors seminar for freshmen and sophomores who hope to become fellowship candidates later in their careers. The course, designed by Bob Graalman, uses current events as a base for classroom discussion. Students become news anchors for a day, summarizing articles and providing their own op-ed about issues addressed by the story. Interview-style rounds of questions follow from faculty and fellow students, challenging their peers' interpretations and suggesting improvements in delivery and logic.

Along with the value of the personal insights inherent in such a course experience, Graalman notes the opportunities for nurturing, for developing skills in speaking, for encouraging more research or public service, for overseas programming, and more. According to Graalman, students can also gain from the personal analysis applications like the Truman can inspire: "And all of which, in my view, came out of the NAFA movement by way of Truman as a way to share more information with students and the result of which was sharing more information with one another as well."[11]

Such classes may or may not include the final and highly personal question on the Truman application (discussed in Chapter 8): "What additional information do you wish to share with the Truman Scholarship Foundation?"[12] While worded with some ambiguity, this question is essential to a process of active self-reflection that allows the student applicant to tell a review committee who they are and why they care about the issues they want to change. For all students—regardless of applicant status or year in school—a question like this is essential for understanding who they are, how they experience the world around them, and who they hope to become. A question like this is often the first question in a job interview—"Tell us a little about yourself and why you are interested in this position." It is perhaps one of the most difficult questions to answer and one that can be most revealing. Learning early about how to respond in ways that are authentic and relevant is an important life skill for any student.

At a celebration of the Truman Foundation's fortieth anniversary in 2016, a panel of distinguished Truman Scholars gathered to share their experiences with the application process and their careers in public service.[13] The panel included Stacey Abrams (MS '94, former member of the Georgia House of Representatives), Chris Coons (DE '83, U.S. Senator from Delaware), Susan Rice (DC '84, former U.S. National Security Advisor), and John King (NJ '95, former U.S. Secretary of Education). During their forty-five-minute conversation, these prominent public figures spoke candidly and appreciatively about the ways in which engaging with their applications and the interview process challenged them to assess their values and focus their interests in serving society. Abrams, who admittedly applied knowing only that the scholarship provided $30,000 for graduate school, noted how her experience with the Truman Scholarship process helped her to "rearrange [her] understanding of who [she] could be" and started her thinking that a career as an elected official would place her in a position to advocate for constituents from disadvantaged communities.

The clarifying nature of the Truman application process has been reported more broadly in surveys conducted by the Truman Foundation. In "Having a Winner Every Time in the Truman Scholarship," an essay written by Louis Blair, originally published in *Beyond Winning: National Scholarship Competitions and the Student Experience* (2005) and reprised in this book as "The Truman Scholarship: Having A Winner Every Time" (Chapter 12), Mr. Blair provides strong evidence for the value of the Truman application process, regardless of the outcome. Blair discusses assessments of the application process from nonfinalists to finalists. Regardless of finalist status, a majority of candidates (67–73 percent) reported being "very satisfied" with the application process. The finalists who were surveyed particularly noted the benefits of clarifying their career goals, becoming aware of values and interests, and planning for graduate school.

A 2014 Truman finalist from Duke offered these thoughts about his experience with the process:

> When I applied for the Truman scholarship back in 2014, I was invested in winning. Like many undergrads, I thought that passing through the hoop would give me instantaneous success (and job security!) in an uncertain world. Far from removing uncertainty, the process taught me about how to navigate an uncertain future and shape it to fit my needs. The kind of visioning on the Truman app trained me to mobilize others around my vision of social change. Now, that kind of mobilization is a key part of my work as an artist and educator. The app was a pep talk to the selection committee, but it also ended up being a pep talk to myself.
>
> An unexpected aspect of the process was realizing how my experiences added up and how they formed the ingredients for a meaningful career. I ran my application by a current Truman Scholar who said to me, "The work you do in theater is amazing! You take it for granted since you're living and breathing it, but when you put all your work together it's pretty unique." Setting my goals down on paper and having outside eyes helped me get over Duke imposter syndrome and speak with confidence about my values. Advising from OUSF and from peers let me know that I had people rooting for me.
>
> Lastly, failure was useful for recalibration. On the application, I pitched myself as someone on a path to work for the National Endowment for the Arts since the Truman seemed government-focused. In retrospect, this path didn't really reflect my love for making art. I think the interviewers could see through that veneer, which helped me recognize it as fakery in myself. I could advance equity in theater in more authentic ways, which is exactly what I'm doing now. As a working artist, I have to deal with rejection quite often. It's good to get used to rejection early and gain skills in resilience and adaptability.[14]

Such compelling evidence suggests the power of the Truman application process in helping students understand their authentic identities as agents for social and political change. Employing the Truman application in early advising—in a student's first or second year—would be a valuable exercise that could motivate all students as they start planning their academic path. Used in this way, the Truman Scholarship application would be a tool for "democratizing the process" and provide students the opportunity to think about their choices long before applying for postgraduate scholarships.

Conclusion

So much that has enriched the academic and engaged learning culture surrounding scholarship applications at our universities in the past two decades started with Truman and with NAFA. And many of the innovations that our universities and academic enhancement programs have initiated in these twenty years, it can be argued, sprang into full bloom because of the vital role the Truman Foundation took in supporting advisors. Indeed, the profession of scholarship advising owes a debt of gratitude to the Truman Foundation for developing tools for advisors and sharing them widely to provide greater access not only to the benefits of the scholarship, but also to the benefits that students derive from the application process. As NAFA and the scholarship advising profession have grown, the impact that this work has had on institutions across the country has also grown. Indeed, the synergies that scholarship advising has sparked and the realization of the value of such a High-Impact Practice has transformed many campus cultures in many places across the U.S. Because of this dynamic partnership, greater numbers of students are engaging in a higher degree of self-reflection and are being introduced to more transformative experiences and tools. And as educators, advisors know the myriad ways the Truman Scholarship application inspires us to take personal inventory of our own larger charge to be "change agents." So, thank you, President Truman, for providing our nation a living memorial that has become "a beacon for public service for young people across the United States" and also a banner and inspiration for all of us as educators. We are in your debt.

Appendix A

The Truman Scholarship Application

I, _____ have read and understand the conditions of the Truman Scholarship as explained in the current *Notes to Candidates for Scholarships* and the current Bulletin of Information. I affirm that I plan to pursue a career in public service as defined in those documents. I give permission to officials of my institution to release transcripts of my academic record and other information requested for consideration in the Truman Scholarship program. I understand that this application will be available only to qualified people who need to see it in the course of their duties. I waive the right to access letters of recommendation written on my behalf. If selected as a Truman Scholar, I agree to attend the Truman Scholar Leadership Week and Awards Ceremony, in Liberty and Independence, Missouri. I affirm that all of this application, including the policy proposal, is my own work for formally cited from other sources. I affirm the information contained herein is true and accurate to the best of my knowledge and belief.

Date _____   Signature _____

Legal name in full
(Print/Type)

Last Name	First Name	M.I.

Permanent residence

_____
Number, Street, and Apartment Number

City		State	ZIP

Your address at school
(if different)

_____
Number, Street, and Apartment Number

City (if studying abroad, add country)		State	ZIP

How is permanent residence established?   Home telephone (   ) _____
(At least two must apply.)

☐ Home address for school registration   School telephone (   ) _____
                                                 (if different)

☐ Place of registration to vote
                                                 E-mail address
☐ Family's primary residence   _____

☐ Other: _____   Age at deadline _____

(Check one) I am a   ☐ U.S. citizen   ☐ U.S. national   ☐ Resident alien expecting citizenship by the date of award

Will you be studying away from your institution during the spring semester?   ☐ Yes   ☐ No

(If yes) Where? _____

Appendix B

The Truman Scholarship Review Rubric

Truman Nominee Rating Form – 12 Point Max

Nominee _____ State _____ Reader _____

	0	1	2	3	Points
Rating Points					
Public Service record and commitment (Items 2, 3, 4, 8, letter)	☐	☐	☐	☐	_____
	☐	☐	☐	☐	
Leadership record (Items 2, 3, 4, 7, letters).					
	☐	☐	☐	☐	_____
Appropriateness for proposed graduate study (Items 3, 6, 10, 11, 12, 13, transcript, policy proposal, letters)					
	☐	☐	☐		_____
Quality of Application: consistency of responses, quality of writing, good picture of the candidate and his/her motivation for a career in public service					
	☐	☐			_____
Bonus.					_____

Point Total: _____

	YES	NO
Essential characteristics for advancement met?		
Enthusiastic and responsive Institution Nomination Letter...	☐	☐
	☐	☐
Sustained participation in two or more of the following...		
▸ Campus activities & student government (Item 2)		
▸ Community activities (Item 3)		
▸ Partisan politics and campaigns (Item 4)		
▸ Government internships or government employment (Items 4, 5)		
▸ Public or nonprofit boards/commissions, public interest/advocacy groups (Items 4, 5)		
	☐	☐
Transcript--Fall semester shows strong grades, ambitious curriculum, and course(s) related to proposed career field		
	☐	☐
Policy-related ambitions in the public sector or in primary/secondary education		
	☐	☐
Graduate study proposal appropriate for career goals and ambitions		
	☐	☐
Consistent responses to Items 9, 10, 11, 12, 13		
	☐	☐
Policy proposal reveals understanding of a significant problem in candidate's intended field *and* some ability to analyze a complex topic		

Overall:

☐   **Outstanding** (Generally, over 8 points)

☐   **Strong** (Generally, 7.0. to 8.0 points)

☐   **Good** (Generally, 6.0 to 6.5 points)

☐   **Not a Finalist** (Generally, fewer than 6 points or no strong case made for advancement)

Comments (Rationale for advancing the candidate/not advancing the candidate.)

Notes

Editors' Note: Several articles in this volume have appeared in earlier NAFA proceedings published by the University of Arkansas Press. They are listed here in the order they appear in the volume: Andrew Rich, "Public Service, Power, and the Challenges Facing Future Public Servants," was first published in *Roads Less Traveled and Other Perspectives on Nationally Competitive Scholarships* under the title "Public Service, Power, and the Challenges Facing Millennials" (2017), 11–17; Tara Yglesias, "The Truman Scholarship Community: Unconventional Scholarship Serving the Public Good," in *Nationally Competitive Scholarships: Serving Students and the Public Good* (2007), 91–97; Andrew Rich, "Broadening Horizons and Building Community: The Truman Foundation's Summer Institute," in *All In: Expanding Access through Nationally Competitive Awards* (2013), 13–17; Tara Yglesias, "Suspenders and a Belt: Overpreparation and the Overachiever," in *Roads Less Traveled and Other Perspectives on Nationally Competitive Scholarships* (2017), 41–19; Tara Yglesias, "Non Ducor, Duco: Leadership and the Truman Scholarship Application," in *Leading the Way: Student Engagement and Nationally Competitive Awards* (2009), 9–17; Tara Yglesias, "I Love It When a Grad Plan Comes Together: Graduate School Advising and the Truman Application," in *All Before Them: Student Opportunities and Nationally Competitive Fellowships* (2015), 25–39; Tara Yglesias, "Enough about Me, What Do You Think about Me? Surviving the Truman Interview," in *All In: Expanding Access through Nationally Competitive Awards* (2013), 19–31; Tara Yglesias, "You Sank My Fellowship: The 'Near-Miss' Truman Application," in *Bridging the Gap: Perspectives on Nationally Competitive Scholarships* (2019), 65–83; Louis Blair, "The Truman Scholarship: Having a Winner Every Time," which appeared as "Having a Winner Every Time in the Truman Competition" in *Beyond Winning: National Scholarship Competitions and the Student Experience* (2005), 33–40. All the essays have been updated to reflect currently existing programs and scholarship requirements and goals.

Chapter 1

1. Public Law 93–642 is available online on the govinfo web page: https://www.govinfo.gov/content/pkg/STATUTE-88/pdf/STATUTE-88-Pg2276.pdf.

2. Jocelyn Kiley, "In Polarized Era, Fewer Americans Hold a Mix of

Conservative and Liberal Views," *FactTank: News in the Numbers (Pew Research Center),* October 23, 1917, https://www.pewresearch.org/fact-tank/2017/10/23/in-polarized-era-fewer-americans-hold-a-mix-of-conservative-and-liberal-views/.

3. John Granlich, "Far More Americans Say There Are Strong Conflicts Between Partisans Than Between Other Groups in Society," *FactTank: News in the Numbers (Pew Research Center),* December 19, 2017, https://www.pew research.org/fact-tank/2017/12/19/far-more-americans-say-there-are-strong -conflicts-between-partisans-than-between-other-groups-in-society/.

4. Susannah Fox, "The Future of the Internet as Baby Boomers Age," *FactTank: News in the Numbers (Pew Research Center),* October 17, 2005, https://www.pewresearch.org/internet/2005/10/17/the-future-of-the-internet-as-baby -boomers-age/.

5. Eric Katz, "The Federal Agencies Where the Most Employees Are Eligible to Retire," *Government Executive,* June 18, 2018, https://www.govexec.com /pay-benefits/2018/06/federal-agencies-where-most-employees-are-eligible -retire/149091/.

6. William H. Whyte, *The Organization Man* (Philadelphia, PA: University of Pennsylvania Press, 1956).

Chapter 4

1. This essay is adapted from a talk given at the Summer 2016 NAFA Regional Conference in Washington, DC, "Public Service and Nationally Competitive Scholarships—Government, Social Activism, Research and Advocacy." The views expressed are those of the author and do not represent any institutional positions by the Truman Foundation.

2. I worked with millennials while serving as executive secretary of the Truman Foundation, but in connection to public service the two generations are closely aligned. See Pew Research Center, January 17, 2019, "Generation Z Looks a Lot Like Millennials on Key Social and Political Issues."

3. Pew Research Center, March 2014, "Millennials in Adulthood: Detached from Institutions, Networked with Friends." See also: Pew Research Center, "On the Cusp of Adulthood and Facing an Uncertain Future: What We Know about Gen Z So Far."

4. Matthew Green, "How Millennials Voted in the 2016 Presidential Election," *KQED News,* November 15, 2016. Generation Z voted in a presidential election for the first time in 2020, and the preliminary numbers seem to be encouraging.

5. "Monthly Unemployment Rate in the United States from December 2015 to December 2016," Statista, the Statistics Portal.

6. Emily Jane Fox, "Suddenly, Millennials Are Dying to Work on Wall Street Again," The Hive, *Vanity Fair,* June 6, 2016.

Chapter 5

1. TB's moment in the Truman application sun coincided with the publication of Tracy Kidder's *Mountains Beyond Mountains*, a book focused on Dr. Paul Farmer's efforts to fight TB in Haiti; Net-a-Porter added "jumpsuits" as a category in 2014.

2. Danielle Paquette, "What We Mean When We Say Hillary Clinton Overprepared for the Debate," *The Washington Post*, September 27, 2016.

3. See *National Lampoon's Vacation* (1983).

4. But the foundation did notice that the problem of being overprepared was more frequent at schools that were also NAFA members. This tendency is likely a function of NAFA schools being generally more invested in preparation.

5. I like to imagine it is *Rime of the Ancient Mariner*.

6. The overuse of "That is a great question, Dr. X" is a fine example of this behavior.

7. Caroline Beaton, "Why Millennials Are So Stressed and What to Do about It," *Psychology Today*, September 5, 2015.

8. Millennials were a stressed generation and now Gen Z is even more so. See The Harris Poll for the American Psychological Society, which indicates that stress levels seem to be higher for Gen Z in 2020 than any other generation.

9. Again, the foundation is sensitive to the pressure that some offices have placed upon them to produce deliverables, either in terms of materials or interviews. But while advisors may have others dictating the workload, they can exert some control over the level of stress the material places on their students.

10. Fear not, the Truman Foundation did not escape the audit either. It reviewed its written materials and left most intact, striking a balance between providing too much information to students who must already sift through a ton of material and being the sole provider for those students without strong advisors.

11. I would be remiss to not make one of my favorite points here: It is extremely rare that someone is made a Truman Scholar because of one discrete thing. We select based on a totality of circumstances and often rely on impressions that are difficult to communicate outside of the interview selection room.

12. Candidates also seem to believe it is appropriate to tell the panel how it stacked up compared to their practice sessions. A general "this interview was not as bad as my practices" is fine, if ill-advised, but providing the interview panel with an assessment of how their questions rate compared to the ones from campus interviews just encourages a panelist to try even harder to stump the candidate.

13. Most of the panelists are not academics.

Chapter 6

1. "I am not led, I lead." This is the city motto of Sao Paulo, Brazil. An expansive definition of leadership would necessarily require that we look to the people who perfected the bikini for guidance.

2. This material is adapted from a 2007 NAFA conference presentation. Thanks to Jane Curlin, Mary Denyer, and Scott Henderson for participating in that presentation and providing many of the best ideas outlined in this essay.

3. This number typically represents a much smaller number of schools since many faculty representatives request information on more than one candidate.

4. The foundation receives approximately 750 applications per year. This number is fairly constant, in part because colleges and universities are limited to only four applications per school (excluding transfer students). We review over 300 files annually.

5. The text of the question is as follows: "Describe one specific example of your leadership. Limit to 2,000 characters including spaces."

6. These questions ask for a listing of high school and college activities, public and community service activities, and political or governmental activities.

7. Question 8 asks students to describe a compelling example of their public service.

Chapter 7

1. The text of Question 11: *Describe the graduate education program you plan to pursue if you receive a Truman Scholarship.*

2. I reviewed my application for this article. The essay was officially *not bad*. It was dry and generic but overall fine.

3. Word choice is a struggle here. Sometimes, the advising is ineffective—the faculty advisor does not provide appropriate feedback and advice. Other times, the student is the problem and either will not or cannot process good advice when given. *Unsuccessful* seemed to capture both of these circumstances.

4. These proposals are extensive. The foundation requires a narrative that covers how this graduate school program fits into the scholar's career objectives, complete curriculum for the program including professors with whom the scholar plans to work, a plan for internships and summer work, a comparison of this program with other similar programs, as well as information about how many graduates from the school go into public service upon graduation. More details are found here: http://www.truman.gov/graduate-school-proposal.

5. All suggestions are entirely doable in your copious free time.

6. Also remember that scholars can defer their scholarship for at least four years after they graduate college. So students who are certain they want to work for several years—or who are not even certain when they will attend graduate school—are still eligible.

7. Truman selection panels are not really like this description. But if the perception helps to motivate students to do a little introspection, so be it.

8. A copy of the form can be found here: http://www.truman.gov/nominee-rating-form.

9. The term *reader* refers to the members of our Finalist Selection Committee. This committee makes the initial cut of applications and determines who will be named a finalist. Once students are named finalists, they are interviewed by the members of the regional review panels—referred to as "panelists."

10. Which sets up Question 14 to be dessert. This arrangement sounds about right as 14 is sometimes perfect and other times entirely too much.

11. For the foundation, the jury is still out on whether these degrees prepare students for careers in public service. It is a rare student for whom the MBA—as opposed to a PhD, MA, MPA/MPP, MUP, or any other public service–oriented degree—would be the best option. Additionally, the track record of scholars who attend business school is mixed at best.

While we are on this subject, MPP versus MPA is not a debate worth having. The difference in program seems to have more to do with when the program was established and the research of current faculty members than anything else. Please see Yongbeom Hur and Merl Hackbart, "MPA vs. MPP: A Distinction without a Difference?" *Journal of Public Affairs Education* 15, no. 4: 397–424; http://www.naspaa.org/jpaemessenger/article/v15n4-hur.pdf.

Chapter 8

1. See, for example, *The Haunting of Hill House* (1959).

2. See, for example, Azathorth AKA "a primal horror too horrible for description," *The Dreams in the Witch House* (1932).

3. Thanks to the poetry of Antonin Scalia in Arizona v. United States (2012).

4. Through the course of feedback and appeals, I likely review one-third to one-half of all applications not selected for interview. I remember very few responses to Question 14.

5. "Personal" was originally added to discourage students from writing essays about their thoughts on public service—something that is still unhelpful. But then applicants assumed that "personal" meant that the essay was not to discuss academic or work accomplishments. Thus a number of students opted not to discuss something of potential interest to the committee in favor of a personal (and often confessional) essay. The foundation removed the word to avoid this confusion.

6. "Optional" was removed to encourage all applicants to complete this section. The foundation noticed that students from institutions with advisors tended to complete this section regardless of whether it was necessary to the application. Students from institutions without tended to leave it blank. The

foundation hoped that by removing it, everyone would at least include some information in this section.

7. This text is the complete question as seen in the student application. On the PDF version of the printed application seen by the readers, the question is shortened to "Additional Information." The readers are aware the text is different.

8. A bonus point is also included on the application rating form. Again, the purpose is to allow those students who may not fit neatly within other categories to participate fully in the competition. A sample of the score sheet is located here: https://www.truman.gov/nominee-rating-form.

9. During this dark time before the National Association of Fellowships Advisors (NAFA), there were many more institutions that fit into this category.

10. For the initial two decades of the Truman Scholarship when the foundation selected scholars as sophomores, it ran a parallel application process open to community college students. When the foundation moved to junior year selection in the early 1990s, it folded those students into the main competition and asked them to apply after completing an associate's degree. But the community college students were often older, returning students, and making sure they were able to compete on even footing with traditional Truman applicants was baked into the use and guidance behind Question 14.

11. If I were really invested in my horror theme, I would go into detail about the fearsome Code of Federal Regulations (unhinged screaming intensifies).

12. The current list includes race, color, national origin, religion, sex, age, genetic information, disability, marital status, pregnancy, economic status, or sexual orientation. The foundation is concerned with diversity across selection institutions, majors, and proposed graduate plans, among other items, even though these items are not the sort of diversity recognized by statute.

13. As a result, the foundation mostly engages in barrier analysis—looking to see who does not apply for the award and why. From there, the foundation tries to make the award more accessible to different types of students.

14. Time for the once-an-article reminder: There is no one thing that makes or breaks a Truman application.

15. Keep in mind that, as a merit-based scholarship, Truman cannot make decisions based solely on need.

16. How to determine whether to let a sleeping B- lie will be discussed later in this essay.

17. Around Halloween, I like to gather the young employees of the Truman Foundation in a darkened room and describe how the foundation used to actually cut and paste applications. Spine-tingling thrills for everyone.

18. His revelation? Flashcards, outlines and highlighters. It was like a whole world of office supplies suddenly opened for me.

19. These ideas might not all have been good ones.

20. The foundation sometimes gets applicants with strong leadership and

solid academics, but without the service piece. They are not good candidates for Truman.

21. To be fair, the concept of "changing the meter" of a story through conflict and setback dates back to Aristotle's *Poetics*. I do not know why I re-read Aristotle's *Poetics* this year, but here we are.

22. Questions 11 through 13 are where we ask the applicants to trace their paths through graduate school and beyond.

23. Associate's degree or equivalent.

24. Panel secretaries (currently Dr. Babcock-Lumish and myself) will often cut off a line of questioning that they feel has become too personal. Applicants should also feel free to do the same, but the foundation understands a reluctance to do so.

25. For example: One woman wrote her entire application about feminism. Her essays were academic and detached. During her interview, it became apparent she was genuinely struggling with her views in the context of her very traditional family as well as her faith. It became difficult for her to discuss these issues, even rhetorically, in the interview room. In that instance, it might have helped for a recommender to alert the foundation that she was in the midst of struggling with these issues herself or for her to make a Question 14 answer that provided more insight in where she was personally. As it was, the interviewers blundered unaware into what was a very painful topic for her.

26. Or will it? (Sinister laughter, fade to black).

Chapter 9

1. Throughout this essay the term *panelist* describes a member of a Truman regional review panel. The panels meet at locations throughout the country to interview finalists and select Truman Scholars. *Reader* describes a member of the Truman Finalist Selection Committee. The Finalist Selection Committee meets prior to the regional review panels and selects finalists based on the written application.

2. See "Practice Questions for Truman Interviews," Truman Foundation website, http://truman.gov//for-faculty-reps/from-the-foundation/practice-questions-for-truman-interviews; the current Bulletin of Information is available on the Truman website in the "For Faculty Reps" section under the current year's competition information.

3. A question the foundation often receives is whether this portion of the day counts as part of the interview process. This session is so short and the interactions so perfunctory that it would be nearly impossible for a finalist to make a lasting impression—either positive or negative. Finalists should not worry about this portion of the day. If they meet the panelists, fine. If not, they will have ample time during the interview.

4. Again, this is not fatal. One recent Truman Scholar closed his interview

with a screed against the Truman process on his campus. According to him, several wonderful Truman candidates were turned away because his campus relied too heavily on GPAs. Several panelists were upset that he used this forum to air his grievances, but they voted to select him anyway.

5. See "Regional Review Panels," Truman Foundation website, http://www.truman.gov/for-candidates/regional-review-panels.

Chapter 10

1. Additional finalists—about 35 in all—are chosen through the appeals process.

2. I am indebted to Elizabeth Veatch, a longtime Truman National Screening Committee member, for her valuable contributions to this essay.

3. See https://www.truman.gov/candidates/regional-review-panels.

Chapter 11

1. I once had a student try to convince me that the allowance for early graduation did not apply to the student because "early" is a relative term.

2. As much as I enjoyed the recent film *Spider-Man: Into the Spider-Verse*, all I could think about was how many "with great power comes great responsibility" quotations I would be seeing this cycle.

3. Once the term *change agent* made its way into the world of venture capitalism, the foundation was in for trouble.

4. I am just as guilty as anyone. I once gave a presentation entitled "Common Truman Mistakes in 10 Minutes or Less or Your Pizza is Free!" To be fair, I was only given ten minutes.

5. This category of application would include those that are incomplete or filled out in such a way that it is apparent neither the student nor the advisor reads any materials relating to selection. As recently as a decade ago, these applications comprised about 10 percent of our total applicant pool.

6. Annually this translates into feedback on approximately a third of the files not selected for interview. The feedback process begins after scholars are announced and continues roughly until the next application launches (April to August).

7. I am leaving "they" deliberately vague as it is often unclear whether the advisor feels this issue was a failing of their student or of their advising.

8. Consider this my annual warning about using successful applications as samples for future applicants. Some Truman Scholars were selected *in spite of* their materials, and advisors cannot know which scholars those might be.

9. A controversial application would be split decisions where one reader votes to advance and the other does not. There is no subject matter or activity

that would be deemed controversial by the selection panels. They have indeed seen everything.

10. There is likewise no assessment by the readers as to whether an issue is important or not. If the student finds an issue compelling, the issue is compelling enough to advance. Readers do not rank or suggest topics suitable for advancement.

11. Residence for the Truman is demonstrated by meeting two of these three options: 1. Home address for school registration (most schools have both a family home and a local address on file for a student); 2. Parent's home address; and 3. Place of registration to vote. For students who choose to vote from their school address, they can now have some flexibility about the state they choose.

12. The foundation also recognizes that there are sometimes external pressures to nominate certain specific or specific types of students. If this issue persists on a particular campus, the advisor may wish to invite a Truman representative for a visit or videoconference to discuss criteria.

13. Readers often read the applications over Valentine's Day weekend. Do with that information what you will.

14. The fact that an application is selected on appeal is not transmitted to the interview committee. Once appeals files are added to the interview pool, the designation is removed, and the file is treated the same as any other.

15. The foundation has attempted to keep the appeals process from candidates in an effort to prevent lobbying for the institution's appeals slot. Much like any good secret, however, most applicants are aware of the process. Advisors may need to consider how and whether to discuss the appeals process with their candidates.

16. The actual reader instructions tell them not to make the case for the student, that is why the foundation has appeals.

17. Students have, for the most part, been working in a writing format where brevity is not prized. Just getting them to stop the bloat is a huge step. After that, work on jargon and clichés.

18. Questions 2 (campus activities), 3 (community service activities), and 4 (government activities).

19. Actual responses and reader critiques can be found at https://www .truman.gov/effective-and-ineffective-responses.

20. One of the Harry Truman quotations the foundation often emblazons on t-shirts is: "It is amazing what you can accomplish if you do not care who gets the credit." Excellent life advice translates into ineffective application advice.

21. For those thinking it will be covered in a letter of recommendation, keep in mind that the application is read first. Readers could make up their minds about the level of leadership before ever getting to the letters. Also, readers are specifically instructed that the letters are to confirm, not supplant what is in the application.

22. Speaking—slowly!—as a former intercollegiate debater, a big wake-up call was looking at graduate school applications and realizing that if I stuck with debate, I would have one activity to write about.

23. A copy can be found here: https://www.truman.gov/nominee-rating-form.

24. Thanks to Dr. Andrew Rich, former executive secretary of the foundation, for giving this category a much punchier name (even if he did want to talk about power all the time).

25. This is a game reference, not a suggestion that we take a foray into academic dishonesty.

Chapter 13

1. For more information on the history of NAFA, see Beth Power's article, "Expanding Access through Organized Support: The History and Purpose of the National Association of Fellowships Advisors," in *All In: Expanding Access through Nationally Competitive Awards* (Fayetteville, Arkansas: University of Arkansas Press, 2013), 119–126.

2. John Dewey, *How We Think*. (Lexington, MA: D C Heath, 1909).

3. Dewey, 2–3.

4. George Kuh, "High-Impact Educational Practices: What They Are, Who Has Access to Them, and Why They Matter," (AAC&U, 2008) is excerpted at https://www.aacu.org/leap/hips.

5. Karen Weber and Ben Rayder, "Early Research Program as a Pathway for Nationally Competitive Scholarships," in *Bridging the Gap: Perspectives on Nationally Competitive Awards* (Fayetteville, AR: University of Arkansas Press, 2019), 11–28.

6. Richard J. Light, *Making the Most of College: Students Speak their Minds* (Boston, MA: Harvard University Press, 2004).

7. Light, 88.

8. See Appendix B in this volume.

9. Mary Tolar, personal email communication, February 18, 2020.

10. Dewey, 3.

11. Robert Graalman, personal email communication, January 28, 2020.

12. For a detailed analysis of Question 14, see Tara Yglesias's "When the Abyss Stares Back: The Eldritch Horror of the 'Additional Information' Prompt," in this volume, Chapter 8.

13. This can be viewed online at https://vimeo.com/trumanscholar.

14. Kari Barclay, personal email communication, February 13, 2020. Barclay graduated from Duke in 2015 and is currently a PhD candidate in theatre and performance studies at Stanford. More information about her can be found at https://www.kari-barclay.com/bio.

Contributors

Terry Babcock-Lumish, the sixth—and first female—executive secretary of the Truman Foundation, has been involved in the selection of Truman Scholars since 2003. Before joining the Truman Foundation, she led Islay, founded in 2005 to provide strategic guidance for philanthropic foundations and other mission-driven organizations across six continents. Previously, she served as the founding director of public policy at the Roosevelt House Public Policy Institute, dedicated to education, research, and civic engagement, in the historic New York City home of Franklin and Eleanor Roosevelt. Recent years' academic affiliations include the University of Arizona, City University of New York, the University of Delaware, Harvard, Oxford, and West Point. Over the last twenty-five years, she has served in local, state, and federal government for both Democratic and Republican administrations. From 1999 to 2001, she served as a Presidential Management Fellow at the Treasury Department and in the Council of Economic Advisers. She then served as a researcher for two books by former vice president Al Gore. She completed her BS at Carnegie Mellon University, where she was named a Truman Scholar, and earned an MPA in environmental and technology policy as a Lilly Community Assistance Fellow at Indiana University's O'Neill School of Public and Environmental Affairs. She earned her DPhil from the University of Oxford as a Clarendon Scholar.

Louis Blair (d. 2020) devoted his entire professional career to public service. As a staff member for the president's science advisors, he held political appointments in the White House during the Ford and Carter administrations. He worked for the U.S. Senate Committee on Commerce, Science, and Transportation. He consulted for the Organization for Economic Cooperation and Development in Paris, the U.S. Environmental Protection Agency, the Appalachian Regional Commission, and the

Commonwealth of Virginia. For seven years, he conducted research at the Urban Institute on ways to enhance the productivity of state and local governments. He was a fellow in the National Academy of Public Administration and served as the executive secretary of the Truman Foundation from 1989 to 2006. In the course of participating on selection panels for Truman, Marshall, Gates Cambridge, Rhodes, and Coca-Cola scholarships, he interviewed nearly four thousand promising young people. More recently, he served as the Mary Moody-Morthen visiting professor at Virginia Military Institute. He then retired to his farm in Virginia, remaining active in numerous ways, including as a mentor to students and advisors until his death in 2020.

Suzanne McCray is vice provost for enrollment services, director of the Office of Nationally Competitive Awards, and an associate professor in the higher education program in the College of Education and Health Professions at the University of Arkansas. For three years, she served on the national program review committee for the Coca-Cola Scholarship; she is in her fourteenth year on the national selection committee for the Morris K. and Stewart L. Udall Scholarship and her fourth for the Critical Language Scholarship. McCray is an active member of the National Association of Fellowships Advisors, serving as its president from 2003 to 2005. During the 2019 national NAFA conference, she was presented with the organization's first service award. She has edited or coedited seven volumes of essays on the topic of nationally competitive scholarships. The most recent is *Bridging the Gap: Perspectives on Nationally Competitive Scholarships* (2019). She earned a BA and an MA in English from the University of Arkansas and a PhD in English from the University of Tennessee.

Jane Coyle Morris is the executive director of the Center for Undergraduate Research and Fellowships at the University of Pennsylvania. In this role, she provides leadership and direction for the office at Penn that supports students seeking research experience and opportunities through nationally competitive scholarships. Prior to her work at Penn, she served as the executive director of Duke's Office of Undergraduate Scholars and Fellows and as director of Villanova's Center for Undergraduate Research and Fellowships. In her leadership roles at Duke and Villanova, she not only directed efforts to broaden participation in nationally competitive scholarships but also managed undergraduate research efforts at Villanova and internal merit scholarship programs at both Duke and Villanova. She is a former president of the National Association of Fellowships Advisors, serving as a direct liaison between the scholarship advisors and the leadership of foundations including Rhodes, Marshall, Mitchell, Truman, and Udall. In this role, she participated directly in helping the Marshall Scholarship Program evaluate and revise their selection criteria to include qualities of intellectual leadership that define excellence in a broader and more meaningful context. She believes deeply in the power of engaging students in an authentic process of discernment, articulation, action, and reflection that moves students from the classroom into postgraduate lives where they can make meaningful contributions to the world. She holds a BS in biology from Villanova University and an MA in biology from Bryn Mawr College, and she spent twenty years as a research scientist before moving into higher education.

Andrew Rich became dean of the Colin Powell School for Civic and Global Leadership at the City College of New York (CCNY) in February 2019. As dean, he oversees the social science departments at CCNY as well as the college's core leadership development and public service programs. Prior to this, he served as executive secretary of the Harry S. Truman Scholarship Foundation beginning in October 2011. Before joining the Truman Foundation, Rich was president and CEO of the Roosevelt Institute, a nonprofit organization devoted to carrying forward the legacy and values of Franklin and Eleanor Roosevelt. He is the author of *Think Tanks, Public Policy, and the Politics of Expertise* (Cambridge University Press, 2004), as well as a wide-ranging number of articles on the role of experts and ideas in the American policy process. He was chair of the political science department at CCNY before joining the Roosevelt Institute. From 1999 to 2003, he taught political science at Wake Forest University. He received his BA from the University of Richmond and his PhD in political science from Yale University. He was a 1991 Truman Scholar from Delaware.

Elizabeth Vardaman retired in the summer of 2019 after a twenty-three-year tenure as associate dean and director of engaged learning for the College of Arts and Sciences at Baylor University in Waco, Texas. An exchange professor in China and assistant director on various Baylor abroad programs in England and the Netherlands in the 1980s and '90s, she traveled extensively on behalf of the university and led the first NAFA tour of British higher education in 2002. Her overview of that trip, "Keys to the United Kingdom," was published in *Beyond Winning: National Scholarship Competitions and the Student Experience*, one of many texts she has published about the scholarship application process. She was a charter member of NAFA and founded the scholarship office for Baylor. In 2017 she chaired a women's symposium at Baylor, and throughout her career has published articles and made presentations on the importance of engaged learning, classroom teaching innovation, and ways students and programs could maximize academic excellence. Baylor established a mentorship award in her name and selected its first seven recipients in spring 2020. That same year, she received the Reynolds Retired Professor award from the university's alumni association.

Paula Warrick, as senior director of the Office of Merit Awards at American University, oversees the university's efforts to mentor candidates for nationally competitive scholarships. She has twenty years of professional experience in the field and has been an active member of NAFA. She served as the organization's fourth president, developed the organization's first strategic plan, and cohosted a regional workshop on scholarships as vehicles for engaging in public service. She has served on the Finalist Selection Committee of the Truman Scholarship for the past several years. She has received awards for her work at American University, including an American University Staff Award for Outstanding Performance.

Tara Yglesias has served as the deputy executive secretary of the Truman Foundation for the past seventeen years and has been involved in the selection of Truman Scholars since 2001. During this time, she had the opportunity to study the trends and characteristics of each incoming class of scholars. She used this knowledge to assist in the development of new Truman Foundation programs and initiatives as well as the design of several new foundation websites and online application systems. She is an active member of NAFA, serving as the Truman Foundation representative to the board for several years, as well as participating in conference planning. An attorney by training, she began her career in the office of the public defender in Fulton County, Georgia. She specialized in trial work and serious felonies but also assisted with the training of new attorneys. A Truman Scholar from Pennsylvania, she also served as a Senior Scholar at Truman Scholars Leadership Week and the Truman Foundation's Public Service Law Conference prior to joining the foundation's staff. She holds a BA in Policy Studies and African American Studies from Syracuse University and a JD from Emory University, where she was a Robert W. Woodruff Fellow.

Index